Lecture Notes in Computer Science

Lecture Notes in Computer Science

Edited by G. Goos and J. Hartmanis

59

Edward Hill, Jr.

A Comparative Study of Very Large Data Bases

Springer-Verlag
Berlin Heidelberg New York 1978

Author

Dr. Edward Hill, Jr.
Division of Computer Research
and Technology
Building 12 A, Room 2041 B
National Institute of Health
9000 Wisconsin Avenue
Bethesda, Maryland 20851/USA

AMS Subject Classifications (1970): 68-02, 68 A 20, 68 A 50, 68 A 99
CR Subject Classifications (1974): 4.33

ISBN 3-540-08653-6 Springer-Verlag Berlin Heidelberg New York
ISBN 0-387-08653-6 Springer-Verlag New York Heidelberg Berlin

Printing and binding: Beltz Offsetdruck, Hemsbach/Bergstr.
2141/3140-543210

PREFACE

This monograph presents a comparison of methods for organizing very large amounts of stored data called a <u>very large data base</u> to facilitate fast retrieval of desired information on direct access storage devices. In a very large data base involving retrieval and updating, the major factor of immediate concern is the average number of accesses to the direct access storage device to complete a request. The average number of accesses to store and retrieve items on a direct access storage device for hashing methods using chaining with separate lists and linear probing is presented. A new algorithm and performance measures for chaining with coalescing lists is presented. New performance measures are presented for storing and retrieving with a binary search tree and a trie stored on a direct access storage device. Algorithms are presented to perform retrieval, insertion, deletion and the inverted file generation operations for an inverted file. New performance measures are presented for an inverted file. The methods are developed using a component concept. A hybrid method involving components is used for the linked files. All methods are analyzed, along with their data structures, to show their effect on the average number of accesses to the direct access storage device while processing a request. Finally, a comparison criterion is developed and each method is compared.

This monograph is based on a D.Sc. dissertation submitted to the Department of Electrical Engineering and Computer Science at The George Washington University in 1977.

ACKNOWLEDGEMENTS

I am indebted to many people who have contributed in a variety of ways to the completion of this monograph.

First of all, I owe a great deal to Prof. A. C. Meltzer who served as my advisor. Prof. A. C. Meltzer deserves thanks for encouraging me to investigate what has now become the topic of this monograph.

Thanks to Dr. Eugene K. Harris and the Division of Computer Research and Technology of the National Institutes of Health, for their support in my studies in Computer Science.

I am indebted to my wife, Espor and my children Eurica and Edward for their love, understanding and support during the many hours this work has kept me from them.

Finally, I am indeed thankful for my parents Edward and Gertrude who sacrificed so much to aid me during the initial years of my career.

TABLE OF CONTENTS

CHAPTER 1

INTRODUCTION

This monograph is a comprehensive investigation of methodology for organizing very large amounts of stored data called a very large data base. This investigation surveys the existing methods and presents a new unified notation and approach for evaluation and comparison of these methods. New storage and retrieval algorithms are designed and developed and performance measures for all methods are established. Comprehensive performance evaluations are carried out for each method as a function of critical design parameters. Comprehensive tables and graphs are presented which permit a direct comparison of method performance. The methodology studied here is designed to facilitate rapid storage and retrieval of information which is stored on a direct access storage device.

In a very large data base involving retrieval and updating, the principle concern is the average number of accesses to the direct access storage device to complete a request. Methods and their associated data structures, are analyzed to show their effect on the average number of accesses to the direct access storage device required to process a request. A comparison criterion is developed and each method is analyzed for a measure of its performance.

The size of a data base may be characterized by the number of entities it concerns and the average number of retrieval terms that apply to information about each entity. A data base in which all pointers, lists and indices reside on a disk is called a very large data base.

Very large data bases are justified only in very large systems, involving many users using large computer complexes and networks. The analysis presented here is concerned with the problem of designing large systems for processing data bases.

High efficency in processing, storage usage, and retrieval is extremely important in processing a very large data base. An inefficient organization of the data base may account for a very large number of disk accesses and result in impractical processing times. The number of disk accesses is strongly connected to the data base data structure and its processing algorithms. The proper data structure and search algorithms will reduce the number of disk accesses, initial load time and data update time.

The approach taken in this monograph is one of synthesis. The simple component parts of various search techniques and their associated data structure are analyzed. These components are used to compare structures for various component organizations. The primary components are files of physical records and addressing mechanisms used to locate records.

The purpose of Chapter 2 is to introduce a set of concepts which is fundamental in defining both a data structure and a search structure for very large data bases. To compare very large data bases, it is essential that each component of the system be well defined. Chapter 2 introduces definitions that give the structures of the data base precise meaning.

Chapter 3 introduces the necessary direct access storage device terminology to analyze algorithms. Since the data base and all pointers are stored on a direct access storage device these terms influence the implementation of any algorithm to search and store records in the data base.

Chapter 4 introduces record processing methods using hashing. The methods analyzed are chaining with separate lists, chaining with coalescing lists and linear probing, denoted by CS, CC and LP respectively. A new search algorithm using coalescing list is introduced and analyzed. New performance measures are presented for chaining with coalescing lists using a general bucket size. A mixture probability distribution is developed to apply the 80-20 rule using the performance measures.

Record processing using tree methods are introduced in Chapter 5. Tree methods are summarized. Algorithms are presented for TREE and TRIE. New performance measures are presented for the TREE and the TRIE. The notation for the TREE and the TRIE is BS and T respectively.

Chapter 6 introduces record processing using linked files, denoted by LL. The component approach used in this monograph is demonstrated. The directory search is by linear probing and the list of files are organized using the chaining with separate list method.

Record processing using an inverted file structure is presented in Chapter 7. The notation used for the inverted file is IF. Algorithms are presented and analyzed for the retrieval, insertion, deletion and inverted file generation operations. New performance measures are presented for an inverted file.

In chapter 8 a criterion for comparison of large data bases is presented. The concepts defined in earlier chapters are used to define various attributes of the comparison criterion. The attribute list is used to define a comparison operator. This comparison operator defines precisely the methods, distribution, relation and other attributes in every comparison.

Chapter 9 presents the conclusions which have been reached on the basis of this research.

CHAPTER 2

DATA BASE STRUCTURE

This chapter defines the record structures and data structures for the data bases used in this monograph. A collection of data, organized in some fashion, is called a data base. Within a data base both organization and content assume importance. Organization of a database consist of the grouping of records and the ordering of records within those groups. This is done to increase the chance of locating known data. It is not enough to know that a particular data item may be in the data base; one must also know how to find it.

Search algorithms are used to locate records in data bases. Two factors that affect search algorithms are the record structure and the data structure of the data base. Basic definitions for a record structure and data structure are presented in this chapter. This is done to explicitly define the notions that are used in later chapters.

2.1.   Record Structure

The basic unit which is processed in a data processing system is called an item or record. An item is made up of two parts: the key and the data. A key K is that part of a record that distinguishes the record from all other records. The length of the key is the number of digits or characters in the key. The data is that part of a record which is not the key. A set of records is a file, and a set of files is called a data_base.

2.2.   Data Structure

The structures discussed here are those relationships that exist between records and files in a data base. Many definitions used are modifications of those in references [10, 20, 35].

The basic unit in a data structure is called a node. A node may consist of a key, data, record, file, or a data base. A structure that involves only linear relative positions of the nodes is called a linear_list. When the list nodes are modified in a way such that one node contains the address of its successor in addition to its normal content , the list is a linked list and the address is called a pointer. A linked list contains a special node to indicate the last node in the list called the termination_node. Most lists are allocated from a linked area of storage called an available storage pool. Therefore, every list must have a pointer to the beginning of the list. A variable (called a link variable) points to the first node of a list and contains the address of the first node of the list. An example of a linked list with a link variable called FIRST is illustrated in figure 2.1.

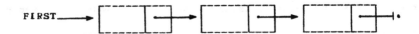

FIRST

Figure 2.1. Linked List.

A special node in a list located at the beginning of the list, is called a <u>list head</u>. Many times it is necessary to organize a list where in the last node points to the first node. Such a list is called a <u>circular linked list</u>. In a circular linked list, sometimes called a <u>ring list</u>, it is a common pratice to include a list head node. The list head node is useful in many search algorithms using lists, because it indicates a node with known attributes.

Often, it is necessary to have two pointers in each node. A list with two pointers in each node, where one points to the node predecessor called the <u>left link</u> (LLINK) and the other points to the node successor called the <u>right link</u> (RLINK), is called a <u>double linked list</u>. An example of this structure is presented in figure 2.2.

Figure 2.2. Doubly Linked Lists.

For large files the lists tend to be long, and extended searches may be required if the list length is not controlled. In all lists discussed so far the list lengths were unrestricted and each list had one starting point. By restricting the list

lengths it is possible to create sublists, each of which has
its own starting point. If the starting points are placed in
an index, the resulting structure is a _partially inverted
list_. When one restricts the list length to one, and places
each key in the index, the index points directly to the record
sought and the resulting structure is called an _inverted
list_.

The advantages and disadvantages of these methods
are not stated in this chapter. These points are analyzed in
chapter 8.

2.3.   _Available Space Management_

The file area is divided into parts called buckets,
which are numbered sequentially throughout the area. Each
bucket has a fixed length, consisting of one or more hardware
blocks.

A track or block level of addressing is assumed
to contain one or more buckets. That is to say, the track
is the lowest level of physical addressing within the file.
The overflow area is a common linked bucket area.

It is assumed that any read or write to the direct
access storage device moves at least one track of information.
The read operation points to the next track to be read in the
case of a multi-track read.

An available track bit mask is used to indicate
the status of tracks. Tracks are allocated by changing the
associated bit to an in use state. Any track that is not
being used has a free bit state associated with it.

CHAPTER 3

DIRECT ACCESS DEVICES

A direct access storage device is one on which each
physical record has a discrete location defined by a unique address.
There are several types of direct access storage devices. The actual
form of the recording surface and the relationship between the
read/write heads and the recording surface determine the type. The
types are:

1. Magnetic drums

2. Magnetic disks, fixed head

3. Magnetic disks, movable head

4. Magnetic cards/strips.

Hardware is not discussed in this monograph. The intent of
this chapter is to introduce the common terminology on direct access
storage devices that are used in this monograph.

3.1. Direct Access Terminology

Many of the definitions which follow are adaptations of
those in references [1, 32, 34]. When the operating system is asks
to retrieve or locate an item on a direct access device, the
electronics instructs the device to move an arm called the access
arm, which contains a read/write mechanism called a read/write head,
to the surface where the data is stored. Once this is done, a data

transfer occurs. The data is kept on a number of rotating surfaces, covered with magnetic material. The individual surface is divided into concentric rings called <u>tracks</u>. One entire track of data passes a read/write head every time the surface completes one revolution. A collection of tracks, which can be read or written without repositioning the access arm, is called a <u>cylinder</u>.

The transfer of data is affected by many factors; however, only the seek time, head switching time, and rotational delay or latency time are considered. Once a device has been selected, some form of mechanical movement may be necessary to access data on a part of the recording surface. This movement will depend on the type of device. Arm position- ing is required on those devices with movable heads. The time E required to move the heads of a device into position to make a transfer is called the <u>seek time</u>. After the heads are placed in position over a required track, it may be necessary to activate a particular head. The time A to activate a particular head is called the <u>head switching</u> time. All direct access storage devices have a recording surface that is rotated under or opposite a series of read/write heads. Any built in delay time D caused by surface rotation is known as <u>rotational delay, or latency</u> time.

Data may be transfered from a direct access storage device once it has been located. This leads to another factor that affects the time required to retrieved or locate an item. The time T required to read or write an item of data is called the <u>transfer rate</u>.

CHAPTER 4

RECORD PROCESSING USING HASHING METHODS

In this chapter we are given a key K, for a record and a
key-to-address transformation, that generates an address used in the
storage or retrieval of that record on a direct access storage
device. We desire to analyze the storage or retrieval of records
regarding all record information stored on a direct access device.

Several methods are summarized. A new search algorithm
using a coalsecing list is introduced and analyzed.

4.1.   Record Addressing Terminology

The definitions presented here are modifications of those
found in [13, 34, 45, 54]. Normally the direct access storage device
space in which identified records are stored is partitioned so that
several records are combined in one storage block. We use the name
bucket for such a block. The bucket size b is the maximum number of
records that can be contained in a bucket. A bucket can be thought
of as being divided into slots. Each slot is designed to hold one
data record. Therefore, the ratio of the active keys to the total
slots available in all buckets is called the load factor.

A key-to-address transformation $h(K)$, sometimes called a
hashing function, maps from the key space into the bucket address
space. We want $h(K)$ to give a uniform random distribution while

mapping K into the bucket addresses. After generating an address h(K) the address is used to enter the address space. This entering of the address space with h(K) is called probing. When the same h(K) is used to enter the address space more than one time, the sequence is called a probe sequence.

The address h(K), where K is the key, is called the home address. Any distinct keys that are mapped into the same bucket slot are called synonyms. Such an occurrence is called a collision at the home address. If a one-to-one map can be constructed then the function is said to be a direct addressing function. When the number of records in a bucket exceed the bucket size we have an overflow. In many cases the overflow records are kept in a common area called an overflow area.

Heising [27] suggested that in many commerical applications, 80 percent of retrievals affect only the most active 20 percent of a file. This rule suggest that a file may have high or low activity in subsets of the file.

Severance and Duhne [65] presented a method to estimate the expected number of accesses required to find a record for arbitrary activity level and subset sizes. Severance and Duhne used two probability distributions to determine another probability distribution called mixtures.

Assume that within the high or low activity subset of the file, all record retrievals are equally likely. Let X be a random variable that is Poisson. Consider a two bucket problem. The random variable X is assigned to one of the buckets with mean m_1 and to the other with mean m_2. Let p_1 be the probability of hitting one of the buckets. This implies that the probability of hitting the other

bucket is $1 - p_1$. The mixture probability is

$$P(X = k) = p_1 \frac{m_1^k e^{-m_1}}{k!} + (1 - p_1) \frac{m_2^k e^{-m_2}}{k!} .$$

The expected value is

$$E(X = k) = \sum_{k=0}^{\infty} kP(X = k)$$

$$= \sum_{k=0}^{\infty} kp_1 \frac{m_1^k e^{-m_1}}{k!} + \sum_{k=0}^{\infty} k(1 - p_1) \frac{m_2^k e^{-m_2}}{k!}$$

$$E(X = k) = p_1 m_1 + (1 - p_1)m_2.$$

For any function $C(k)$ we have

$$E(C(k)) = \sum_{k=0}^{\infty} C(k)P(X = k).$$

So,

$$E(C(k)) = p_1 \sum_{k=0}^{\infty} C(k) \frac{m_1^k e^{-m_1}}{k!} + (1 - p_1) \sum_{k=0}^{\infty} C(k) \frac{m_2^k e^{-m_2}}{k!}$$

$$= p_1 \bar{C}_{m_1} + (1 - p_1) \bar{C}_{m_2}.$$

Let x be the proportion of the data records which receive high

activity. Let y be the proportion of accesses directed to high

activity records. Define

$$p_1 = \frac{y - x}{1 - x} .$$

This implies that

$$(1 - p_1) = \frac{1 - y}{1 - x} .$$

Define

$$E(C(k)) = \tilde{C}_\delta(\alpha, b, x, y),$$

$$\bar{C}_{m_1} = \bar{C}_\delta(\alpha x, b) \text{ and }$$

$$\bar{C}_{m_2} = \bar{C}_\delta(\alpha,b),$$

where $\tilde{C}(\alpha,b,x,y)$ is the average number of buckets accessed for the mixture, α is the load factor, b is the bucket size and δ is either the retrieval, insertion or deletion operation. The expected number of buckets accessed for the mixture is

$$\tilde{C}_\delta(\alpha,b,x,y) = \frac{y - x}{1 - x} \bar{C}_\delta(\alpha x,b) + \frac{1 - y}{1 - x} \bar{C}_\delta(\alpha,b),$$

where

$$\delta = \begin{cases} R & ,\text{retrieval} \\ I & ,\text{insertion} \\ D & ,\text{deletion} \end{cases}$$

b is the bucket size and α is the load factor.

When $x = .2$ and $y = .8$ we have the 80-20 rule.

Define N to be the number of uniquely identified records to be stored. Let d be the number of buckets for N records. Assume that we have an equal probability of assigning a record to any of the available buckets. In this case we have N records and d buckets. The number of records k assigned to a bucket will have a binomial probability distribution with parameters $1/d$ and N.

$$\beta(k;N,1/d) = \binom{N}{k}(1/d)^k (1 - 1/d)^{N-k}$$

Feller [21] presented an approximation to the Poisson distribution by the binomial distribution. This approximation is now presented in terms of the notation used in this monograph. Define $\frac{N}{d} = m$ to be the average number of records assigned to a bucket. For $k = 0$ we

have

$$\beta(0;N,\tfrac{m}{N}) = (1 - \tfrac{m}{N})^N.$$

Taking the logarithm of both sides and using the Taylor expansion,

we find

$$\log \beta(0;N,\tfrac{m}{N}) = N\log(1 - \tfrac{m}{N}) = -m - \tfrac{m^2}{2N} - \dots$$

For large N

$$\beta(0;N,\tfrac{m}{N}) = e^{-m} + O(N^{-1}).$$

For any fixed k and sufficiently large N

$$\frac{\beta(k;N,\tfrac{m}{N})}{\beta(k-1;N,\tfrac{m}{N})} = \frac{m-(k-1)(\tfrac{m}{N})}{k(1-\tfrac{m}{N})} \approx \frac{m}{k}.$$

Therefore,

$$\beta(1;N,\tfrac{m}{N}) = m \times \beta(0;N,\tfrac{m}{N}) = me^{-m},$$

$$\beta(2;N,\tfrac{m}{N}) = \tfrac{m}{2} \times \beta(1;N,\tfrac{m}{N}) = \tfrac{m^2}{2} e^{-m},$$

and in general by induction

$$\beta(k;N,\tfrac{m}{N}) \approx \frac{m^k e^{-m}}{k!}.$$

This is the Poisson approximation to the binomial distribution.

Denote this probability distribution by

$$P(k) = \frac{m^k e^{-m}}{k!},$$

where m is the average number of records assigned to the buckets.

The Poisson distribution gives the fraction of the addresses to which

exactly k keys will be transformed for a random distribution with an

average of m keys per address.

4.2.   Chaining_With_Separate_Lists

Collisions may be resolved by chaining all synonyms on a list. Each list has its head located at the home address. All lists are organized in buckets to store them effectively on a direct access storage device. Whenever more than b records fall into the same bucket, a link to an overflow record is inserted at the end of the first bucket. All overflow records belonging to a certain bucket are organized in a chain in the overflow area.

The node structure for chaining with separate lists is illustrated in figure 4.1.

```
 _____
|         |         |
|  NODE   |  LINK   |
|_____|_____|
```

NODE   is the count of the bucket size

LINK   is a pointer to the list of keys in this

       bucket.

a.   HEAD node structure

```
 _____
|      |      |          |
| INFO | TAG  |  LINK    |
|_____|_____|_____|
```

INFO   is the stored key.

LINK   is a pointer to the list of keys in the

       current bucket when NODE $\neq$ 0. When NODE

       is zero it is a pointer to a list in the

       overflow area.

$$\text{TAG} = \begin{cases} 0 \text{ node is a BUCKET node.} \\ \\ 1 \text{ the pointer points to an overflow node.} \end{cases}$$

b.   BUCKET and OVERFLOW node structure

Figure 4.1.   Node Structure for Chaining With

       Separate Lists Algorithm.

4.2.1.   Retrieval_Algorithm

Algorithm   (Retrieval by hash chaining with separate

          lists.)

          Assume that BUCKET is a linked available storage pool

pointed to by a link vector AVAIL. BUCKET is linked in such a way

that the nodes of the buckets are linked together. Assume that

OVERFLOW is a linked available storage pool pointed to by the link

variable OVAIL. The variables P and Q are link variables. The

variable P moves along the list and the variable Q follows P. A

key-to-address transformation h(K) is used to transform the keys into

bucket addresses. The functions NODE, LINK, TAG and INFO operate on

the nodes of the data structure pointed to by the link variable. The

variable i is an auxiliary variable used in the algorithm. Define

READ(P) to mean the reading of a track from the disk containing the

address P. f is a function that maps track addresses into internal

main memory addresses.

```
[Hash the key.]
          GET K,
          i←h(K), i←READ(i), i←f(i).
[Is there a key stored at the home address?]
          IF (LINK(HEAD(i)) = 0)
                THEN  DO PUT "not found", STOP ENDDO.
[There is a list at the home address.]
                ELSE P←f(LINK(HEAD(i))).
          ENDIF.
[Check the list for the current key.]
          DO
[Check for the end of the list.]
              IF (P = 0)
                    THEN  DO PUT "not found", STOP ENDDO.
              ENDIF.
              IF (TAG(P) = 1)
                    THEN  DO P←LINK(P), P←READ(P), P←f(P),
                              IF (OVERFLOW(P) = K)
                                    THEN  DO PUT "found",
                                              STOP ENDDO.
                              ELSE  DO Q←P, P←f(LINK(Q))
                                    ENDDO.
```

```
                    ENDIF.
                 ENDDO.
        ELSE    IF (BUCKET(P) = K)
                    THEN    DO PUT "found", STOP
                        ENDDO.
                    ELSE    DO Q←P, P←f(LINK(Q))
                        ENDDO.
                ENDIF.
        ENDIF.
    ENDDO.
```

4.2.2.   <u>Retrieval Time</u>

Johnson [33] defined the total number of probes required

to address all items in a list of k items as

$$t_k = k + \frac{1}{2} ((k - b)(k - b + 1)),$$

where $k > b$.

The number of records is N and the number of buckets is d.   Assume

equal usage of records, the distribution of list lengths in the

chaining method reduces to the binomial distribution for k successes

in N independent trials with probability $\frac{1}{d}$ of success at each

trial.   In this case k is the list length.   Since $\frac{1}{d}$ is small

and N is large for any typical file, the Poisson approximation to the

binomial distribution can be applied.   The probability $P(k)$ of a list

length k is

$$P(k) = \frac{\lambda^k e^{-\lambda}}{k!} ,$$

where $\lambda = \frac{N}{d}$.

The Poisson distribution has a mean

$$\sum_{k=0}^{N} kP(k) = \lambda.$$

The length of a list is the number of records in a list.   The mean

list length is λ.   Hence $\lambda = m$, the average number of records in a

bucket.   The expected value of the number of probes per item addressed is the mean number of probes per list divided by the mean number of items per list. This yields

$$\bar{C}_R(\alpha,b) = \frac{\sum\limits_{k=0}^{N} t_k P(k)}{\sum\limits_{k=0}^{N} k P(k)} \quad ,$$

where b is the bucket size, α is the load factor and

$$P(k) = \frac{m^k e^{-m}}{k!} \quad .$$

$$\bar{C}_R(\alpha,b) = \frac{1}{m} \sum\limits_{k=0}^{N} t_k P(k).$$

Substituting for t_k yields the average number of accesses

$$\bar{C}_R(\alpha,b) = 1 + \frac{1}{2m} \sum\limits_{k>b}^{N} (k^2 - 2kb + k + b^2 - b)\frac{(\alpha b)^k e^{-\alpha b}}{k!}.$$

Consider the special case where b = 1. Substituting this value for b and rewriting the above equation yields

$$\bar{C}_R(\alpha,1) = 1 + \frac{1}{2} \sum\limits_{k-1=1}^{N} (k-1)\frac{m^{k-1} e^{-m}}{(k-1)!} \quad ,$$

$$\bar{C}_R(\alpha,1) = 1 + \frac{m}{2} \quad .$$

This result was first presented by Johnson [33] and later by others [27, 47, 48, 55]. Another chaining method called block chaining was introduced by Collmeyer [17].

4.2.3. Insertion Algorithm

Algorithm   (Insertion by hash chaining with separate

lists.)

Assume that BUCKET is a linked available storage pool pointed to by a link vector AVAIL. BUCKET is linked in such a way that the nodes of the bucket are linked together. Assume that OVERFLOW is a linked available storage pool pointed to by the link variable OVAIL. Define R$\leftrightarrow$AVAIL[i] to be the removal of a node from the available storage pool and the final management of the AVAIL pointer and underflow conditions. Define R$\leftrightarrow$OVAIL to be the removal of a node from the available storage pool in the overflow area and the final managemant of the OVAIL pointer and underflow conditions. The variables P, Q and R are link variables. The variable P moves along the list and the variable Q follows P. A key-to- address transformation h(K) is used to transform the keys into bucket addresses. The functions NODE, LINK, TAG and INFO operate on the nodes of the data structure pointed to by the link variables. The variable i is an auxiliary variable used in the algorithm. Define READ(P) to mean the reading of a track from the disk containing the address P. Define WRITE(P) to mean the writing of a track on the disk containing the address P. f is a function that maps track addresses into internal main memory addresses.

```
[Hash the key.]
          GET K.
          i←h(K), i←READ(i), i←f(i).
[Is there a key stored at the home address?]
          IF (LINK(HEAD(i)) = 0)
                    THEN  DO
[There is no list. Start a list using this key.]
                              R←AVAIL[i],
                              LINK(HEAD(i))←R,
                              INFO(f(R))←K,
                              LINK(f(R))←0,
                              NODE(HEAD(i))←NODE(HEAD(i))-1,
                              WRITE(R), STOP ENDDO.
[There is a list at the home address.]
                    ELSE  P←f(LINK(HEAD(i))).
          ENDIF.


          DO
[Check the list for the current key.]
              IF (TAG(P) = 1)
                    THEN  DO P←LINK(P), P←READ(P), P←f(P),
```

```
                              IF (OVERFLOW(P) = K)
                                    THEN   DO PUT "found",
                                              STOP ENDDO.
                                    ELSE   DO Q←P,
                                              P←f(LINK(Q)) ENDDO.
                              ENDIF.
                         ENDDO.
                 ELSE   IF (BUCKET(P) = K)
                              THEN   DO PUT "found", STOP
                                         ENDDO.
                              ELSE   DO Q←P, P←f(LINK(Q))
                                         ENDDO.
                         ENDIF.
            ENDIF.
[Check for the end of the list.]
            IF (P = 0)
                  THEN DO
[The key is not in the list. Insert the key into
 the list.]
                              IF (NODE(HEAD(i)) = 0)
                                    THEN   DO R≟OVAIL,
                                              TAG(f(R))←1,
                                              TAG(Q)←1
                                           ENDDO.
                                    ELSE   DO R≟AVAIL[i],
                                              NODE(HEAD(i))←
                                              NODE(HEAD(i))-1
                                           ENDDO.
                              ENDIF.
                         ENDDO.
            ENDIF.
                         LINK(Q)←R,
                         LINK(f(R))←0,
                         INFO(f(R))←K,
                         WRITE(f^{-1}(Q)), WRITE(R),
                         STOP
            ENDDO.
```

4.2.4.   Insertion Time

An item is inserted by first performing a retrieval

operation. If the item is in the structure a notification is given

about its presence. If the item is not in the structure it is

inserted.

The insertion time is that time required to determine if

the item is in the file. The item is in the bucket d or it is on a

chain associated with the home address in the overflow area. The average number of accesses to the direct access storage device during an insertion operation is

$$\bar{C}_I(\alpha,b) = 1 + \sum_{k>b}^{\infty} (k - b)P(k) \quad .$$

The unsuccessful search was presented by Knuth [34] as

$$C_N' = 1 + \sum_{k>b}^{\infty} (k - b)\frac{(\alpha b)^k e^{-\alpha b}}{k!},$$

where C_N' is the average number of file accesses in an unsuccessful search. This unsuccessful search is defined to be the insertion time.

4.2.5.   Deletion Algorithm

Algorithm (Deletion by hash chaining with separate

              lists.)

Assume that BUCKET is a linked available storage pool pointed to by a link vector AVAIL. BUCKET is linked in such a way that the nodes of the bucket are linked together. Assume that OVERFLOW is a linked available storage pool pointed to by the link variable OVAIL. Define AVAIL[i]$\Leftarrow$P to be the return of a node to the available storage pool and the final management of the AVAIL pointer and overflow conditions. Define OVAIL$\Leftarrow$P to be the return of a node to the available storage pool in the overflow area and the final management of the OVAIL pointer and overflow conditions. The variables P and Q are link variables. The variable P moves along the list and the variable Q follows P. A key-to-address transformation h(K) is used to transform the keys into bucket addresses. The functions NODE, LINK, TAG and INFO operate on the nodes of the data structure pointed to by the link variable. The variable i is an auxiliary variable used in the algorithm. Let LOC be a function that returns the address of a variable. Define READ(P)

to mean the reading of a track from the disk containing the address

P. Define WRITE(P) to mean the writing of a track on the disk

containing an address P. f is a function that maps track addresses

into internal main memory addresses.
[Hash the key.]
```
        GET K,
        i←h(K),  i←READ(i),  i←f(i).
[Is there a key stored at the home address?]
        IF (LINK(HEAD(i)) = 0)
                THEN  DO PUT "not found", STOP ENDDO.
                ELSE  Q←LOC(HEAD(i)).
        ENDIF.
[There is a list at the home address.]
        P←f(LINK(HEAD(i))).



        DO
[Check the list for the current key.]
        IF (TAG(P) = 1)
                THEN  DO P←LINK(P), P←READ(P), P←f(P),
                        IF (OVERFLOW(P) = K)
                                THEN  DO LINK(Q)←LINK(P),
                                        OVAIL≜f⁻¹(P),
                                        WRITE(LINK(Q)),
                                        STOP ENDDO.
                                ELSE  DO Q←P,
                                        P←f(LINK(Q))
                                      ENDDO.
                        ENDIF.
                      ENDDO.
                ELSE  IF (BUCKET(P) = K)
                                THEN  DO LINK(Q)←LINK(P),
                                        AVAIL[i]≜P,
                                        WRITE(LINK(Q)),
                                        STOP ENDDO.
                                ELSE  DO Q←P,
                                        P←f(LINK(Q))
                                      ENDDO.
                      ENDIF.
        ENDIF.
[Check for the end of the list.]
        IF (P = 0)
                THEN  DO PUT "not found", STOP ENDDO.
        ENDIF.
        ENDDO.
```

4.2.6.   Deletion Time

Deletions in this structure are performed by initiating a

retrieval operation. The average number of accesses required to locate an item is $\bar{C}_R(\alpha, b)$.

The average number of accesses to the direct access storage device is the same as that for the retrieval operation. This average is $\bar{C}_D(\alpha, b)$.

4.2.7.   Storage Space Requirements

The amount of storage required by the buckets is bd words. Assume that a word is large enough to hold a key and a pointer.

Hence, the average storage requirement presented by van der Pool [55] and denoted by ω_c is

$$\omega_c = bd + d \sum_{k > b}^{\infty} (k - b)P(k).$$

4.3.   Chaining with Coalescing Lists

4.3.1.   Retrieval And Insertion Algorithm

Lists generated by storing a new record in a free slot of any unfilled bucket when the home address is occupied and linking this new bucket to the current chain of the home address are called coalescing lists. This technique processes each record only once when it first enters the system. An algorithm, due to Knuth and Williams [34, 70], is a convenient way to solve the problem using tables in memory. Our tables are large so we desire an algorithm that allows the information to be placed on a direct access storage device. Algorithm A is a convenient way to solve the problem using coalescing chaining within buckets.

Algorithm A   (Double chained scatter table search and insertion)

This algorithm searches a double chained list of buckets,

of size b looking for a given key K. If K is not in the bucket and
the bucket is not full, K is inserted. If the bucket is full, the
key is placed on a list with a header pointed to by H. New buckets
are taken from a list of available space pointed to by AVAIL. The
current bucket being filled is pointed to by a pointer called ROVER.

The basic unit of BUCKET is called a node. The nodes of
the buckets are denoted by BUCKET[i], for $0 \leq i \leq b$, and they
are of two distinguishable types, empty and occupied. An occupied
node contains a key field INFO[i], a link field LINK[i], and possible
other fields. Each bucket has a distinguishable first node and last
node whose key fields are LLINK[ROVER] and RLINK[ROVER]
respectively. An illustration of the node structure of the
coalescing list is given in figure 4.2.

LLINK	c	NODES	RLINK

a. Node Structure Of A Bucket.

INFO[i]	INFO	LINK

b. Node Structure Of A List

Figure 4.2. Coalescing List Node Structure.

This algorithm makes use of a hash function h(K). An auxiliary variable R is used, to help find empty spaces; when the bucket is empty, use R=ROVER+b. The variables SS and GS are link variables. The last node of the last filled bucket and the last node of the bucket currently being filled are pointed to by SS and GS respectively. The list are allowed to coalesce within each bucket, and BUCKET[j] is occupied for all j in the range R $\leq$ j $\leq$ ROVER.

```
A1.   [Initialize pointers.]
          IF (H = 0)
              THEN  DO ROVER←AVAIL, AVAIL←RLINK[AVAIL],
                      GS←ROVER+b, RLINK[GS]←0, SS←H,
                      RLINK[H]←ROVER, R←GS,
                      LLINK[ROVER]←SS, SS←R ENDDO.
          ENDIF.
A2.   [Hash.]  j←h(K)+1.  (Now 1 ≤ j ≤ b.)
A3.   [Are there any full buckets?]
          IF (R = ROVER ∧ RLINK[GS] ≠ 0)
              THEN  DO ROVER←RLINK[GS], i←j+ROVER,
                      R←ROVER+b, go to A4 ENDDO.
          ELSE  i←j+ROVER.
          ENDIF.
A4.   [Is there a list?]
          IF (BUCKET[i] is empty)
              THEN  DO Mark BUCKET[i] as an occupied
                      node, with INFO[i]←K and
                      LINK[i]←0, STOP ENDDO.
          ENDIF.

          (The BUCKET[i] is occupied: we will look at
          the list of occupied nodes within the bucket which
          starts here).
          DO
A5.   [Compare.]  IF (K = INFO[i])
                        THEN  DO PUT "found", STOP ENDDO.
                  ENDIF.
A6.   [Advance to next.]
          IF (LINK[i] ≠ 0)
              THEN  i←LINK[i]
              ELSE  go to A7.
          ENDIF.
          ENDDO.


A7.   [Find empty node.] (The search was unsuccessful
          and we want to find an empty position in the bucket).
          Decrease R one or more times until finding a value
```

```
            such that BUCKET[R] is empty.
            IF (R = ROVER ∧ RLINK[GS] = 0)
                THEN   IF (AVAIL = 0)
                            THEN   DO PUT "overflow",
                                   STOP ENDDO.
                            ELSE   DO ROVER←AVAIL,
                                   AVAIL←RLINK[AVAIL],
                                   R←ROVER+b, GS←R,
                                   RLINK[R]←0,
                                   RLINK[SS]←ROVER,
                                   LLINK[ROVER]←SS,
                                   SS←R, i←j+ROVER,
                                   go to A4 ENDDO.
                    ENDIF.
            ENDIF.
            IF (R = ROVER ∧ RLINK[GS] ≠ 0)
                THEN   DO ROVER←RLINK[GS],
                          R←ROVER+b, GS←R, i←j+ROVER,
                          go to A4 ENDDO.
            ENDIF.
            LINK[i]←R, i←R.
   A8.  [Insert new key.]  Mark BUCKET[i] as an occupied
        node, with INFO[i]←K and LINK[i]←0
```

Several lists are allowed to coalesce, so that records need not be
moved after they have been inserted into buckets.

4.3.2.   Retrieval Time

Knuth [34] presented results for calculating the retrieval
time using coalescing lists for a bucket size of one. Severance and
Duhne [65] in a summary of addressing methods presented the same
results. A new method is presented here that uses a general bucket
size for a coalescing list.

Assume an equal probability of assigning a record to any of
the available buckets. There are N items stored by chaining with
coalescing lists in d buckets. The load factor is

$$\alpha = \frac{m}{b},$$

where

$$m = \frac{N}{d}.$$

For N, d → ∞ keeping m constant we have,

$$P(X = k) = P(k) = \frac{m^k e^{-m}}{k!}.$$

In the retrieval process each record on the direct access storage device is equally likely to be the record which we seek. The address $h(K)$ defines the home address where the search begins.

A list may partially fill a bucket, fill it exactly, or overflow the bucket. Knuth [34] concluded that the list of occupied nodes tend to be short when lists are allowed to coalesce. The contribution to total list length due to coalescing must be small to keep the total list length short. Assume that the number of probes required to address all items due to coalescing is

$$\frac{(k - b)}{2} \quad .$$

Define the total number of probes required to address all items in a list of k items as

$$t_k = k + \frac{1}{2}(k - b)(k - b + 1) + \frac{(k - b)}{2} \quad .$$

where $k > b$.

The expected value of the number of probes per item addressed is the mean number of probes per list divided by the mean number of items per list. This yields

$$\bar{C}_R(\alpha, b) = \frac{\sum_{k=0}^{N} t_k P(k)}{\sum_{k=0}^{N} k P(k)} \quad .$$

The average number of accesses is

$$\bar{C}_R(\alpha, b) = 1 + \frac{1}{2m} \sum_{k>b}^{N} (k^2 - 2kb + k + b^2 - b) \frac{(\alpha b)^k e^{-\alpha b}}{k!}$$

$$+ \frac{1}{2m} \sum_{k>b}^{\infty} (k - b)P(k) \quad .$$

The special case $b = 1$, yields

$$\bar{C}_R(\alpha,1) = 1 + \frac{m}{2} + \frac{1}{2} - \frac{1}{2m} + \frac{e^{-m}}{2m} .$$

Knuth [34] presented a result for chaining with separate lists for b = 1, as

$$C_N = 1 + \frac{1}{8\alpha}(e^{2\alpha} - 1 - 2\alpha) + \frac{1}{4}\alpha ,$$

where C_N is the number of accesses during a retrieval and α is the load factor. The new result presented above for b = 1 approximates Knuth's result with a maximum absolute error of .05, for $.1 \leq \alpha \leq .9$.

4.3.3.   Insertion_Time

The insertion time for coalescing list has not been defined for a general bucket size. A new unsuccessful search for coalescing lists is presented and the insertion time is defined in terms of this search.

Assume the maximum list length in an insertion is

(k - b + 1).

Then, the average number of accesses to a direct access storage device during an insertion is

$$\bar{C}_I(\alpha,b) = 1 + \sum_{k > b}^{N} (k - b + 1)P(k).$$

4.3.4.   Deletion_Algorithm

The key K is used in a retrieval operation. Algorithm A is started at the first step. If the record is not found, nothing is deleted. When the record is found in the search a deletion indicator is inserted for the record. The deletion indicator is inserted by modifying step A5 of Algorithm A. Algorithm A is modified by replacing the PUT "found" by

INFO[i]←deletion indicator

4.3.5. Deletion Time

A deletion is made by initiating a retrieval. If the record is not found, nothing is deleted; otherwise, the record is deleted.

In this case, the average number of accesses to the direct access storage device, denoted by $\bar{C}_D$, is

$$\bar{C}_D(\alpha,b) = \bar{C}_R(\alpha,b).$$

4.3.6. Storage Space Requirements

The amount of storage required to store coalescing lists on a direct access storage device has not been previously presented. The total storage requirement for storing coalescing list on a direct access storage device is presented below.

The average storage requirement presented by van der Pool [55] for chaining with separate lists is defined in terms of the unsuccessful search. The amount of storage required by the buckets is bd. Assume that a node is large enough to hold a key and a pointer. The unsuccessful search for coalescing lists is

$$\bar{C}_I(\alpha,b) = 1 + \sum_{k>b}^{N} (k - b + 1)P(k).$$

The average amount of storage required to store N keys in a coalescing list structure, denoted by ω_l, is

$$\omega_l = bd + d \sum_{k>b}^{\infty} (k - b + 1)P(k).$$

4.4. Linear Probing

One way to resolve the problem of collisions is to do away with the links, and use an open type addressing system with linear probing. An open type addressing system is organized as follows:

there is a set of rules by which every key K determines a probe

sequence; for each acceptable key K, a list of possible memory

positions is inspected whenever the record with K as its key is

inserted or retrieved. Initially the record with key K is normally

stored in the first open position on the list using the probe

sequence determined by K. If the first position is already occupied,

the second position is used. If an open position is encountered

while searching for K, using the probe sequence determined by K, the

conclusion is that K is not in the list, since the same sequence of

probes is made every time K is processed.

Peterson [54] introduced this method and called it open

addressing. Peterson discussed several different types of addressing

systems, and obtained estimates and simulation results for the mean

search time.

4.4.1.   Retrieval Algorithm

Algorithm A´ (Retrieval hashing with linear probing)

A key-to-address transformation h(K) is used to transform

the keys into bucket addresses. The function INFO[i] is used to

retrieve a key from a node of a bucket. Let P be a link variable

that contains the address of a disk track. Define READ(P) to mean

the reading of a track containing the address P. Assume that r is

the address of the first location of a track that has been set by

READ(P). Assume that F is the address of the first location of the

first track containing the directory. Assume that L is the address

of the last location of the last track containing the directory. The

variables i and k are auxillary variables used by the algorithm. f

is a function that maps track addresses into internal main memory addresses.

[Hash the key and read the track specified by
 the address.]
```
            GET K,
            i←h(K),
            i←READ(i), k←i, i←f(i).
            DO
```
[Compare key with current key.]
```
            IF (INFO[i] = K)
                    THEN  DO PUT "found", STOP ENDDO.
                    ELSE  IF (INFO[i] = empty)
                                    THEN  DO PUT "not found",
                                                  STOP ENDDO.
                            ENDIF.
            ENDIF.
```
[Advance to the next position.]
```
            i←i - 1,
            IF (f⁻¹(i) = k)
                    THEN  DO PUT "not found", STOP ENDDO.
            ENDIF.
            IF (i < f(r))
                    THEN DO
```
[Is this the last track before k?]
```
                            IF (f⁻¹(i) < F)
                                    THEN  DO
```
[Move to the tracks after k.]
```
                                            i←L,
                                            i←READ(i), i←f(i),
                                          ENDDO.
                            ELSE  DO i←READ(f⁻¹(i)),
                                       i←f(i) ENDDO.
                            ENDIF.
            ENDIF.
            ENDDO.
```

4.4.2.   Retrieval Time

Knuth [34] introduced the average number of accesses made

by chaining with separate lists in an unsuccessful search as

$$1 + \sum_{k>b} (k - b)P(k) = 1 + \alpha b t_b ,$$

where α is the load factor and b is the bucket size.

The average number of accesses to the direct access

storage device described by Knuth [34] is

$$\bar{C}_R(\alpha,b) = 1 + t_b(\alpha) + t_{2b}(\alpha) + t_{3b}(\alpha) + \cdots ,$$

where

$$t_{nb}(\alpha) = \frac{\sum\limits_{k \geq nb}^{\infty} (k - nb)P(k)}{\alpha nb} \quad ,$$

α is the load factor, b is the bucket size and n = 1, 2, ...

Schay and Spruth [61] proposed a modification of the open addressing system which removed some of the randomness. They called the new method the modified open addressing system and introduced a Markov chain model for the search time for a bucket size one. The average retrieval time presented was

$$\bar{n} = \frac{1}{2} - \frac{\rho}{1 - \rho} \quad ,$$

where $\bar{n}$ is the average retrieval time and ρ is the load factor.

Morris [48] presented a model for this method which calculates the search time for a bucket size of one without derivation. The average retrieval time presented was

$$E = 1 + \frac{\alpha}{2} \quad ,$$

where E is the average retrieval time and α is the load factor.

Tainiter [67] modified Schay and Spruth method and introduced a Markov chain model for a general bucket size. For buckets of size n solve n linear equations in n unknowns to obtain M_0, M_1, M_2, ..., M_{n-1} from

$$M_n = \frac{M_0 - \sum\limits_{j=0}^{n-1} M_j \sum\limits_{j=0}^{n-j} P_j}{P_0} \quad ,$$

where

$$P_j = \frac{\rho^j e^{-\rho}}{j!} \quad ,$$

and ρ is the average number of records in a bucket. Use the M's to calculate the average retrieval time in

$$P(V_j) = \frac{1}{\rho} \sum_{k=0}^{jn-1} M_k \sum_{v=max(0,(j-1)n-k)}^{jn-1-k} \Gamma_{v+1}(\rho),$$

where $\rho P(V_j)$ is the average retrieval time for the number

of records whose calculated address is i which are in bucket

i + j - 1. ρ is the average number of records in a bucket, n

is the bucket size, j = 1, 2, ... and

$$\Gamma_k(\rho) = 1 - e^{-\rho} \left(\sum_{j=0}^{k-1} \frac{\rho^j}{j!} \right), \ k = 1, 2, ..., \Gamma_0(\rho) = 1.$$

4.4.3. Insertion Algorithm

Algorithm A'' (Insertion hashing with linear probing)

A key-to-address transformation h(K) is used to transform

the keys into bucket addresses. The function INFO[i] is used to

insert a key into a node of the bucket. Let P be a link variable

that contains the address of a disk track. Define READ(P) to mean

the reading of a track containing the address P. Define WRITE(P) to

mean the writing of a track on the direct access storage device

containing the address P. Assume that r is the address of the first

location of a track that has been set by READ(P). Assume that F is

the address of the first location of the first track containing the

directory. Assume that L is the address of the last location of the

last track containing the directory. The variables i and k are

auxiliary variables used by the algorithm. f is a function that maps

track addresses into internal main memory addresses.

```
[Hash the key and read the track specified by
 the address.]
            GET K,
            i←h(K),
            i←READ(i), k←i, i←f(i).
            DO
```

```
[Compare key with current key.]
            IF ( INFO[ i ] = K )
                THEN  DO PUT "found", STOP ENDDO.
                ELSE  IF ( INFO[ i ] = empty)
                            THEN  DO
[Insert the key.]
                                        INFO[ i ]←K,
                                        WRITE( f⁻¹( i )),
                                        STOP ENDDO.
                        ENDIF.
            ENDIF.
[Advance to next position.]
            i←i - 1,
            IF ( f⁻¹( i ) = k )
                THEN  DO
[Overflow condition.]
                            PUT "The table is full",
                            STOP ENDDO.
            ENDIF.
            IF ( i < f( r ) )
                THEN
[Is this the last track before k?]
                    IF ( i < F )
                        THEN  DO
[Move to the tracks after k.]
                                    i←L,
                                    i←READ( i ),
                                    i←f( i ),
                                ENDDO.
                    ELSE  DO i←READ( f⁻¹( i )),
                             i←f( i ) ENDDO.
                ENDIF.
        ENDIF.
        ENDDO.
```

4.4.4.   Insertion_Time

The only measure of performance for linear probing has been
the retrieval time. A measure is presented here for insertion by
linear probing.

An insertion is made by hashing the key and looking for the
key in the file. If the key is not in the file it is inserted;
otherwise, an indication of the key's presence is returned.

The average number of accesses to the direct access storage
device during an insertion is the same as that for the retrieval.
Hence,

$$\bar{C}_I(\alpha,b) = \bar{C}_R(\alpha,b).$$

4.4.5.   Deletion Algorithm

Algorithm A''' (Deletion hashing with linear probing)

A key-to-address transformation h(K) is used to transform the keys into bucket addresses. The function INFO[i] is used to delete a key from a node of a bucket. Let P be a link variable that contains the address of a disk track. Define READ(P) to mean the reading of a track containing the address P. Define WRITE(P) to mean the writing of a track on the direct access storage device containing the address P. Assume that r is the address of the first location of a track that has been set by READ(P). Assume that F is the address of the first location of the first track containing the directory. Assume that L is the address of the last location of the last track containing the directory. The variables i and k are auxillary variables used by the algorithm. f is a function that maps track addresses into internal main memory addresses.

```
[Hash the key and read the track specified by
 the address.]
          GET K,
          i←h(K),
          i←READ(i), k←i, i←f(i).
          DO
[Compare key with current key.]
             IF (INFO[i] = K)
                 THEN  DO
[Insert a deletion indicator for this key.]
                       INFO[i]←deletion indicator,
                       WRITE(f^{-1}(i)),
                       STOP ENDDO.
                 ELSE  IF (INFO[i] = empty)
                          THEN  DO PUT "not found",
                                   STOP ENDDO.
                       ENDIF.
             ENDIF.
[Advance to the next position.]
          i←i - 1,
```

```
              IF ( f⁻¹( i ) = k )
                     THEN  DO PUT "not found", STOP ENDDO.
              ENDIF.
              IF ( i < f( r ) )
                     THEN  DO
[Is this the last track before k?]
                            IF ( f⁻¹( i ) < F )
                                   THEN  DO
[Move to the tracks after k. ]
                                           i←L,
                                           i←READ( i ),
                                           i←f( i ) ENDDO.
                            ELSE  DO i←READ( f⁻¹( i )),
                                           i←f( i ) ENDDO.
                     ENDIF.
           ENDIF.
        ENDDO.
```

4.4.6.   Deletion Time

When a deletion is made it is assumed that the key is
hashed and a search is made for the key in the file. If the key is
found, a deletion indicator is inserted in the key position. This
maintains a steady state for the file. Therefore, the deletion time
is also

$$\bar{C}_D(\alpha,b) = \bar{C}_R(\alpha,b).$$

4.4.7.   Storage Space Requirements

In the linear probing method there is no overflow area.
The total space required, denoted by ω_p, is

$$\omega_p = db.$$

4.5.   Summary

Searches are initiated in response to a query expressed in
relation to the set of all valid records. The hashing methods
discussed in this chapter are good for searches that involve a single
key, and are called simple queries. These methods work by generating
a number, which is influenced by all characters of the key word, and

yet, appears to be random with respect to them. This is extremely difficult when dealing with variable word length information, especially with long words, where only one letter differs or where the letters are the same but two have been interchanged.

The major problems occur when these keys are placed on the disk. In the discussions in this chapter, certain assumptions have been made about storing the keys on direct access storage devices. Changing the assumptions in the methods presented may produce invalid results.

The effect of various track organizations are presented in [53]. This paper presents several decisions on overflow procedures and file organizations that result in acceptable file utilization.

When retrieving records with equal probability Peterson [54] verified that the order in which records are stored in an open addressing method has no effect on the average number of accesses to retrieve a record. Severance and Duhne [65] concluded that reordering has no effect on the average number of accesses in a chaining with separate lists method. Reordering prevents merging of synonym chains in the coalescing chaining method, and initially provides a performance which is equivalent to chaining with separate lists method.

When the data base is large, the number of possible interesting keys is large. For large sets of keys one would like to perform more operations than a simple query on the data base. Several interesting queries are performed on large data bases. Queries that specify that the records to be retrieved are those that intersect some subset of the set of valid records are called intersection queries. A query which asks if a specified record is in the data structure is called an _exact match query_. An intersection query in which values are specified for a proper subset of the keys is called a _partial match query_. The most general type of intersection query is one in which any region may be specified as the set with which the records to be retrieved must intersect, this query is called a _region query_. These queries have been studied in Rivest and Bentley[59, 9].

Other key-to-address transformations and collision resolution methods for tables stored in main memory are described in [3, 6, 7, 11, 12, 18, 39, 44, 45, 58, 63, 64, 68]. Simulations involving large formatted files that are stored on a disk are presented in [40, 41, 42].

CHAPTER 5

RECORD PROCESSING USING TREE METHODS

In this chapter the links of the structures of the keys and records of the very large data base are disk addresses. The keys and data are stored on a direct access storage device, with only a small number of them remaining in main storage at one time.

It is necessary to maintain the ability to find items and change items in the data base economically. Clearly, the speed of finding and inserting items is a function of the arrangement of the data on the disk and the properties of the search, insertion, and deletion algorithms. Maximum speed must be accomplished while maximizing the use of disk storage.

5.1. Tree Searching Terminology

Most definitions in this section are adaptations and modifications of those in references [8, 34, 66]. A directed graph is a set of nodes $N_1, N_2, N_3, \ldots N_n$ and a set of arcs called branches with a specified orientation connecting various pairs of nodes. An example of a simple connected graph is given in figure 5.1.

N_1 N_3

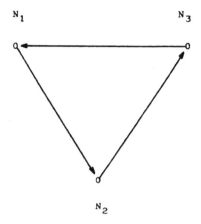

N_2

Figure 5.1. A Directed Graph.

A sequence of branches such that the terminal node of each branch coincides with the initial node of the succeeding branch is called a path. The number of branches in a path is called the length of the path or height of the tree. Any node N_j is reachable from node N_i if there is a path from node N_i to node N_j. A path is closed if its initial node is N_1 and its terminal node is N_i. A path is a cycle $N_1, N_2, \ldots, N_n, N_1$ if its length is at least one and n nodes are distinct. Movement along any path is called a walk.

A tree is a directed graph that has no cycles and has, at most, one branch entering each node. A collection of trees is a forest. Any walk in a tree is a path and, since there are no cycles, it follows that a path existing between any two nodes is unique with unique length.

A root of a tree is a node which has no branches entering it, and a leaf or a terminal node is a node which has no branches leaving it. Any non-leaf or non-terminal node is called a branch_node. A root is said to lie on the first level of the tree, and a node which lies at the end of a path of length j - 1 from a root is on the jth level of the tree. The number of branches leaving a node is called the degree or branching_ratio of that node. These definitions are presented in figure 5.2.

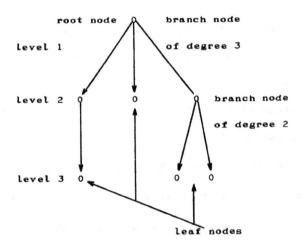

Figure 5.2. A Tree.

The set of nodes which lie at the end of paths of length one from node x comprises the __filial set__ of node x, and x is the __parent__ node of that set. The nodes in the filial set are __siblings__ of each other and the __offspring__ of x. The set of nodes reachable from node x is said to be __governed__ by x and comprises the nodes of the __subtree__ rooted at x. If each node and the subtrees of a tree are simply ordered, then the tree is called an __ordered tree__. In an ordered tree, any path of length k from the root can be uniquely specified by a __vector__.

$$i = (i_1, i_2, \ldots i_k)$$

where i_j indicates the number of branches to be traversed at level j of a specified path. This vector is a unique specification for the terminal node of the path which can be referred to as node i. In figure 5.3, these definitions are presented with an ordered tree whoses branches are ordered from left to right.

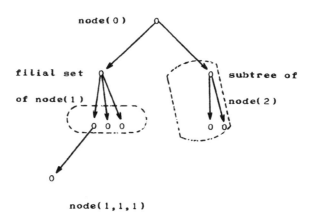

Figure 5.3.   An Ordered Tree.

A tree is <u>balanced</u> if the difference between the path
lengths from the root to any two leaves is at most one. Several
ideas on balanced trees and their reconstruction are analyzed in [23,
31, 36, 37, 51]. A balanced tree is illustrated in figure 5.4.

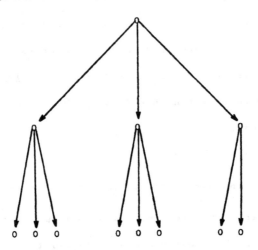

Figure 5.4.   A Balanced Tree.

Hibbard [29] introduced the binary search tree.   A <u>binary</u>
<u>search tree</u> is a directed graph having the following properties:

1.   There is one and only one node, called the root,
     such that for any node p there exist one and
     only one path which begins with the root and
     ends with p.

2. For each node p, the number of links beginning
   with p is either two or zero.

3. The set of links is partitioned into two sets
   L and R. Each link belonging to L is called a
   left link. Each link belonging to R is called a
   right link.

4. For each node p containing two links, there is
   exactly one left link beginning with p and
   exactly one right link beginning with p.

The nodes of a binary search tree contain an information field that may contain one or more digits or characters. There are two types of nodes in a binary search tree. An *internal node* is one with at least one link that is not null. A node with the left link and right null is called an *external node*. Insertions are made into an existing binary search tree as the value of the first blank node found while traversing the tree along some path from the root. At the root and any succeeding node, the branches on a path are taken left if the key is less than the node value or right if the key is greater than the node value. Path terminations are indicated by a blank node. The path length is a function of the sequence in which the key is stored in the binary search tree. This is different from the TREE and the TRIE, where the path length is a function of the length of the key.

The shape of the binary search tree varies. This give rise to search lengths that range from

$$\frac{N + 1}{2}$$

for a binary search tree with only right links or only left links to

$$\log_2 N$$

for a balanced binary search tree. An illustration of a binary

search tree is presented in figure 5.5.

File = {1, 2, -1, -3, 4, -6}

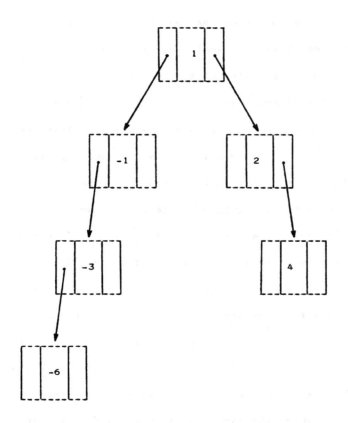

Figure 5.5. Binary Search Tree.

Efficient methods of searching tree structures are proposed by Clampett [15]. Coffman and Eve [16] proposed a general method of file structuring using a hashing function to define the tree structure. Coffman and Eve studied Trees and Binary Search Trees.

Nievergelt [52] presented a survey on binary search trees. He concluded that the main open problems concerning the use of binary search trees for large file organization is their allocation in a two-level store. The mean search time for binary search trees stored on a direct access storage device for a very large file organization is not known. This problem is solved in section 5.2.2.

An M-ary tree whose nodes are M-place vectors with components corresponding to digits or characters is called a trie. This structure was introduced by Fredkin [24]. A trie stores records in its leaves or external nodes. Any node on a given level h represents the set of all keys that begin with a certain sequence of h characters. The node indicates an M-ary branch, depending on the (h + 1)st character.

An example of a trie is illustrated in figure 5.6. The trie of figure 5.6 has ten nodes; node (1) is the root, where the first letter is found. If the first letter is B, node (1) tells us to go on to node (3), looking up the second letter in the same way; node (3) says that the second letter is E.

File = {A, BE, IF, HIM, HAD, HE}

	(1)	(2)	(3)	(4)	(5)	(6)	(7)	(8)	(9)	(10)
	---	A	---	---	---	---	---	HE	---	---
A	(2)	---	---	---	(7)	---	---	---	---	---
B	(3)	---	---	---	---	---	---	---	---	---
C	---	---	---	---	---	---	---	---	---	---
D	---	---	---	---	---	---	HAD	---	---	---
E	---	---	BE	---	(8)	---	---	---	---	---
F	---	---	---	IF	---	---	---	---	---	---
G	---	---	---	---	---	---	---	---	---	---
H	(5)	---	---	---	---	---	---	---	---	---
I	(4)	---	---	---	(6)	---	---	---	---	---
J	---	---	---	---	---	---	---	---	---	---
K	---	---	---	---	---	---	---	---	---	---
L	---	---	---	---	---	---	---	---	---	---
M	---	---	---	---	---	HIM	---	---	---	---

Figure 5.6. A Trie.

Morrison [49] discovered a way to form N-node search trees on the binary representation of keys, without storing keys in the nodes. This method is suitable for dealing with extremely long, variable-length keys.

In many cases, addressing in a trie is related to addressing in a multidimensional array. Hellerman [28] analyzed and generalized the method of addressing in a multidimensional array.

Bayer and McCreight [4] solved the problem of storing keys on a disk by developing what is called a page, a block of storage of fixed size used to transfer information between main storage and direct access storage.

The organization, called a B-tree, used pages as nodes of a tree. Bayer and McCreight introduced a data structure for the B-tree. The data structure included algorithms to insert, retrieve and delete information from the B-tree.

Define $h \geq 0$ to be the height of the tree. Let k denote the least number of records in any node of the tree. A tree T is a B-tree in the class $\tau(k,h)$ of B-trees if T is empty or has the following properties:

1. The length of any path from the root to any leaf is h.

2. Each node except the root and the leaves has at least $k + 1$ sons. The root is empty or it has at least two sons.

3. Each node has at most $2k + 1$ sons.

The node structure and example of a B-tree with k = 1, h = 3 is presented in figure 5.7. The natural numbers are used for keys.

The data part of the B-tree is omitted.

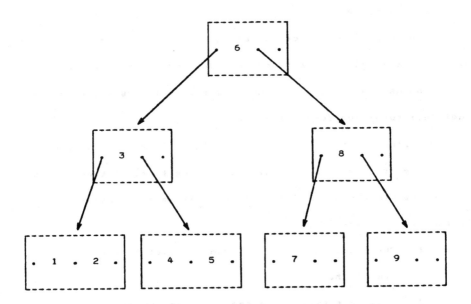

| P_0 | K_1 | D_1 | .... | K_{2k} | D_{2k} | P_{2k} |

P = pointer.
K_i = key.
D_i = data.

a. Format of a B-Tree node.

Figure 5.7. B-Tree.

The pages which are nodes of the B-tree must be allowed to grow. When the pages grow to their maximum length, it is necessary to divide the pages in a systematic way to allow the B-tree to continue to grow. The process of dividing a full page and creating a new page with one part of the page is called splitting_a_page.

B-trees allow retrieval, insertion, and deletion of records in time proportional to $\log_k N$ where N is the number of records and k is a device dependent parameter, such that the performance of the scheme becomes near optimal. It is difficult to derive average performance measures for B-trees. Upper and lower bounds for performance measures have been derived by Bayer and McCreight. Maintenance algorithms have been presented by Bayer [5].

Bayer and McCreight [4] showed that the height h of a B-tree is a variable on which the performance of the three operations mentioned above depends. The bounds on h are

$$\log_{2k+1} (N + 1) \leq h \leq 1 + \log_{k+1} (\frac{N + 1}{2}) ,$$

where $h \geq 1$.

A slight variation of the B-tree is a tree where all data are stored in leaf nodes. Any B-tree in which the non leaf nodes contain only pointers and keys and the data are stored in the leaf nodes is called a B^{*}-tree.

The B^{*}-tree was introduced by Wedekind [69]. Again, it is difficult to derive average performance measures for B^{*}-trees.

Muntz and Uzgalis [50] introduced algorithms to allocate storage for a binary search tree. They approximated the mean number of page transitions in a search of the binary tree.

A track allocation scheme is introduced to store TREE, Binary Search Trees, and TRIE sequentially. Average performance measures are calculated for each structure. The method presented is flexible and efficient. One parameter controls the efficiency which is device dependent.

5.2.   Storing TREE And Binary Tree

Knuth [35] has shown that there is a natural transformation from any tree to a binary tree. It is shown that an internal search algorithm can be modified to search trees on a direct access storage device.

The binary search trees considered in this monograph contain nodes with data and pointers. It is assumed that the data is not all available initially but it is received in some arbitrary order. As the data is received, the tree is generated dynamically.

The critical measure of performance is the average number of accesses to the direct access storage device during a search of the binary search tree. The reference of a track during a search is called a track transition. The average search time is clearly a function of the number of track transitions during a search of the tree. Since the tree is allowed to grow dynamically it is important to allocate the tracks such that the number of track transitions are minimized during a search.

Assume P is a pointer to a track. Introduce a function $f(x)$ that uses P to generate an address within a track where x is the location of a node in a track. The function

$$f(x) = P + x$$

is a one-to-one mapping of a node pointed to in a track which is in the internal main memory buffer. Since the function is one-to-one it has an inverse $f^{-1}(x)$. The inverse $f^{-1}(x)$ is the location of the node in the track P.

An algorithm B is presented to illustrate how an internal search algorithm is modified to retrieve keys from tracks. To reduce storage waste a new node structure is defined and an algorithm is presented that uses the best features of the Briandais [19] method. This algorithm uses the idea presented by Braindais, in which he stated the process of building the TREE can be continued indefinitely. An illustration of the node structure is presented in Figure 5.8.

CODE	INFO	ANEXT	ENEXT

CODE $\begin{cases} - & \text{indicates the end of the string.} \\ \\ + & \text{indefinite continuation indicator.} \end{cases}$

INFO is the stored character.

ANEXT is the address of the next filial set.

ENEXT is the address of the sibling.

a. Format Of A Letter Entry

CODE	ADATA	ENEXT

ADATA is the address of data.

b. Format Of A Word Terminating Entry

PT	CT	ROV

PT   is the pointer to the tree for a particular

letter.

CT   is the number of nodes in the list pointed

to by PT.

ROV   is the upper limit on the number of nodes in

a list pointed to by PT before a continuation

indicator is inserted in the list.

c. Format Of A Root Node

Figure 5.8. Node Structure For Algorithm B.

This structure is more practical since it allows more bits for the address fields, a pointer to the data area associated with the string, and an indefinite continuation field.

Algorithm B (Storage and Retrieval in a Hash Rooted Symbol Tree)

Assume that BUCKET is a large storage pool pointed to by AVAIL. Define $R \rightleftharpoons$ AVAIL to be the removal of a node from the available storage pool and the final management of the AVAIL pointer and underflow conditions. A key-to-address transformation h(K) is used to transform the keys into bucket addresses. The link vector PT is used to keep track of the root of the trees. A switch called SR is used to indicate storage or retrieval. The functions ANEXT, ENEXT, ADATA, INFO and CODE operate on the nodes defined in the data structure pointed to by the link variable. CT is a vector used to store the length of each list pointed to by PT. The vector ROV is used to hold the count of the next continuation for each list pointed to by PT. The link variable R points to the last node removed from AVAIL. A link variable P is used to move along the tree from the root. Q is a temporary link variable used to move along subtrees of a tree. Let c be the maximum length of a list before a continuation indicator is inserted in the list. Let C be the the sequence of characters to be stored or retrieved with index j.

CODE $\begin{cases} - & \text{indicates the end of the string.} \\ \\ + & \text{indefinite continuation indicator.} \end{cases}$

INFO is the stored character.

ANEXT is the address of the next filial set.

ENEXT is the address of the sibling.

ADATA is the address of data.

PT   is the pointer to the tree for a particular letter.

CT   is the number of nodes in the list pointed to by PT.

ROV   is the upper limit on the number of nodes in

      a list pointed to by PT before a continuation

      indicator is inserted in the list.

c   is the length of a list before a continuation.

$$SR = \begin{cases} 0 & \text{store} \\ 1 & \text{retrieve} \end{cases}$$

B1. [Initialize.] GET C, $j \leftarrow 1$, $i \leftarrow h(C_1)$, $P \leftarrow PT(i)$,
     IF $(SR = 1 \wedge P = 0)$
           THEN DO PUT "not found", STOP ENDDO.
     ENDIF.
     IF $(SR = 0 \wedge P = 0)$ THEN go to B9.
     ENDIF.
B2. [Compare characters.] IF $(C_j = \triangledown)$ THEN go to B6.
                         ENDIF.
     IF $(CODE(P) = '+')$ THEN $P \leftarrow ADATA(P)$.
     ENDIF.
     IF $(C_j = INFO(P))$ THEN go to B7.
     ENDIF.
B3. [Check for code.] IF $(CODE(P) = '+')$
                    THEN $P \leftarrow ADATA(P)$.
              ENDIF.
     IF $(CODE(P) = '-')$ THEN go to B5.
     ENDIF.
B4. [Is it a sibling or a filial set node?]
     IF $(ANEXT(P) = 0)$ THEN go to B9.
     ENDIF.
     IF $(ENEXT(P) = 0)$ THEN go to B8.
     ENDIF.
     $P \leftarrow ENEXT(P)$, go to B2.
B5. [Find the next part.] $Q \leftarrow ENEXT(P)$,
     IF $(Q = 0 \wedge SR = 1 \wedge C_j = \triangledown)$ THEN go to B10.
     ENDIF.

```
          IF (Q = 0)  THEN  go to B8.
          ENDIF.
          P ← Q, go to B2.
  B6.  [Last character.] IF (CODE(P) = '+')
                                  THEN P ← ADATA(P).
                            ENDIF.
          IF (CODE(P) = '-')  THEN  go to B10.
          ENDIF.
          IF (SR = 1)  THEN  DO PUT "not found", STOP ENDDO.
          ENDIF.
          R ⇄ AVAIL
          CT(i) ← CT(i) + 1
          IF (CT(i) > ROV(i))  THEN  CON(i).
          ENDIF.
          CODE(R) ← '-',
          ADATA(R) ← ADR,
          ANEXT(P) ← R, STOP.


  B7.  [Look at the next character.] Q ← ANEXT(P),
          IF (Q = 0)  THEN  go to B5.
          ENDIF.
          P ← Q, j ← j + 1, go to B2.
  B8.  [Insert character in sibling node.] R ⇄ AVAIL,
          INFO(R) ← C_j, ENEXT(P) ← R, CT(i) ← CT(i) + 1,
          IF (CT(i) > ROV(i))  THEN  CON(i)
          ENDIF.
          j ← j + 1, P ← R,
          IF (C_j = ▽)  THEN  go to B6.
          ENDIF.
          go to B9.
  B9.  [Store characters.] R ⇄ AVAIL, CT(i) ← CT(i) + 1,
          IF (CT(i) > ROV(i))  THEN  CON(i)
          ENDIF.
          INFO(R) ← C_j, IF (P ≠ 0)  THEN  ANEXT(P) ← R,
          IF (SR = 0 ∧ P = 0)  THEN  PT(i) ← R
          ENDIF.
          j ← j + 1, P ← R,
          IF (C_j = ▽)  THEN  go to B6.
          ENDIF.
          go to B9.
  B10. [Characters found.] AR ← ADATA(P), STOP.
```

Definition of CON(i): CODE(R) ← +, ADATA(P) ← R,

$$P \leftarrow R, \ ROV(i) \leftarrow ROV(i) + c,$$

$$CT(i) \leftarrow CT(i) + 1, \ R \rightleftarrows AVAIL.$$

A typical rooted tree produced by this algorithm is presented in figure 5.9. The nodes in the tree are nodes in BUCKET. All pointers are pointers to nodes in BUCKET and are not disk addresses. A B´ algorithm presented later will show how the modified internal algorithm B is used to retrieve records stored on disk. In this case the links are disk addresses.

After storing CAN, CAND, CANDY, EGG.

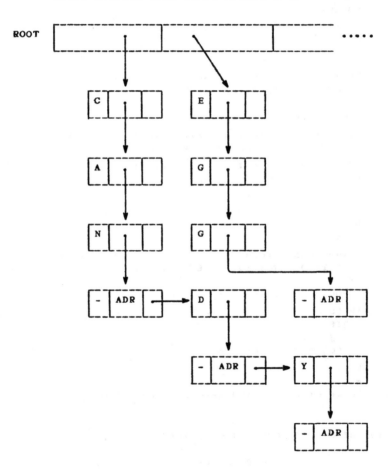

Figure 5.9. Hash Rooted Symbol Tree.

Every tree produced by algorithm B is a binary tree rooted in the forest called ROOT. An illustration of two binary trees rooted in ROOT is presented in figure 5.9.

The nodes of the symbol tree in figure 5.9 must be modified to store the tree on a direct access storage device. In each letter entry node introduce tags ATAG and ETAG in the ANEXT and ENEXT fields respectively. The ETAG is placed in the ENEXT field of the word terminating entry. The ATAG and ETAG tags are defined as follows:

$$ATAG = \begin{cases} 0 & \text{ANEXT is a disk address in another track.} \\ \\ 1 & \text{ANEXT is a pointer within the track.} \end{cases}$$

$$ETAG = \begin{cases} 0 & \text{ENEXT is a disk address in another track.} \\ \\ 1 & \text{ENEXT is a pointer within the track.} \end{cases}$$

The organization of a track is shown in figure 5.10.

File = {A, B, C}

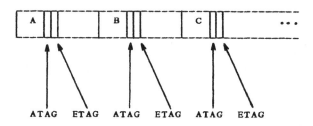

Figure 5.10. Organization Of A Track.

5.2.1.   Retrieval Algorithm

The retrieval algorithm is similar to the old retrieval algorithm B. The tags are used to guide the algorithm within the track and to other tracks. An important point to remember is a tag of zero indicates that the link field contains the address of another track. A special condition occurs when the node contains a termination code and the vector $C_j = \triangledown$. In this case the ADATA field contains the direct access storage address of the data associated with the key contained in C_j.

A modified version of the retrieval part of algorithm B is presented as algorithm B´. This algorithm shows how a typical internal search algorithm is modified to retrieve information from trees stored on a direct access storage device. Define READ(P) to mean the reading of a track from the direct access storage device containing the address P, into an internal main memory buffer.
Algorithm B´ (Retrieval in a hash rooted symbol tree stored

on a direct access storage device.)

The roots of the trees are stored in a link vector called PT. A key-to-address transformation h(K) is used to transform the keys into bucket addresses. The functions ANEXT, ENEXT, ADATA, INFO, CODE, ATAG and ETAG operate on nodes defined in the data structure pointed to by the link variables. The function f maps the track addresses into main memory addresses.

CODE $\begin{cases} - & \text{indicates the end of the string.} \\ \\ \bullet & \text{indefinite continuation indicator.} \end{cases}$

INFO   is the stored character.

ANEXT is the address of the next filial set.

ENEXT is the address of the sibling.

ADATA is the address of data.

PT   is the pointer to the tree for a particular letter.

$$ATAG = \begin{cases} 0 & \text{ANEXT is a disk address in another track.} \\ \\ 1 & \text{ANEXT is a pointer within the track.} \end{cases}$$

$$ETAG = \begin{cases} 0 & \text{ENEXT is a disk address in another track.} \\ \\ 1 & \text{ENEXT is a pointer within the track.} \end{cases}$$

B'1.   [Initialize.] GET C, $j \leftarrow 1$, $i \leftarrow h(C_1)$, $P \leftarrow PT(i)$,
       IF ($P = 0$) THEN   DO PUT "not found", STOP ENDDO.
       ENDIF.
       $P \leftarrow READ(P)$, $P \leftarrow f(P)$.
B'2.   [Compare characters.] IF ($C_j = \triangledown$) THEN go to B'6.
       IF (CODE(P) = '+')
               THEN   IF (ATAG(P) = 0)
                               THEN DO $P \leftarrow READ(ADATA(P))$,
                                         $P \leftarrow f(P)$ ENDDO.
                               ELSE $P \leftarrow f(ADATA(P))$.
                       ENDIF.
       ENDIF.
       IF (C_j = INFO(P)) THEN go to B'7.
       ENDIF.
B'3.   [Check for code.]
       IF (CODE(P) = '+')
               THEN   IF (ATAG(P) = 0)
                               THEN DO
                                         $P \leftarrow READ(ADATA(P))$,
                                         $P \leftarrow f(P)$ ENDDO.
                               ELSE $P \leftarrow f(ADATA(P))$.
                       ENDIF.
       ENDIF.

```
              IF (CODE(P) = '-') THEN  go to B'5.
B'4.   [Is it a sibling or a filial set node?]
       IF (ETAG(P) = 0)
              THEN DO P ← READ(ENEXT(P)), P ← f(P) ENDDO.
              ELSE P ← f(ENEXT(P)).
       ENDIF.
       go to B'2.
B'5.   [Find the next part.]
       IF (ETAG(P) = 0)
              THEN  DO Q ← READ(ENEXT(P)),
                        IF (Q ≠ 0) THEN Q ← f(Q) ENDDO.
                        ENDIF.
              ELSE  Q ← f(ENEXT(P)).
       ENDIF.
       IF (Q = 0 ∧ C_j = ▽) THEN  go to B'8.
       ENDIF.
       P ← Q, go to B'2.


B'6.   [Last character.]
       IF (CODE(P) = '+')
              THEN  DO IF (ATAG(P) = 0)
                            THEN  P ← READ(ADATA(P)),
                        P ← f(P) ENDDO.
                            ENDIF.
              ELSE  P ← f(ADATA(P)).
       ENDIF.
       IF (CODE(P) = '-') THEN  go to B'8.
       ENDIF.
       PUT "not found", STOP.
B'7.   [Look at the next character.]
       IF (ATAG(P) = 0)
              THEN  DO Q ← READ(ANEXT(P)),
                        IF (Q ≠ 0) THEN  Q ← f(Q)
                        ENDIF.
                    ENDDO.
              ELSE  Q ← f(ANEXT(P)).
       ENDIF.
       IF (Q = 0) THEN  go to B'5.
       ENDIF.
       P ← Q, j ← j + 1, go to B'2.
B'8.   [Characters found.] AR ← ADATA(P), terminate.
```

This algorithm is more efficient in terms of search speed
than the one presented by Bayer and McCreight for large data bases.
In the Bayer and McCreight method the keys are ordered in pages of
the B-tree. This requires a linear search of the keys to find a
particular key in a page. The search length for this search is

63

$\underline{2k \pm 1}$. They suggested the use of a binary search in
2

the page for large sets of keys. A binary search is faster with a

search length of $\log_2 2k$. Remember, there is a price of ordering the

keys when the binary search is used. The Bayer and McCreight method

cannot solve the problem solved using algorithm B′ economically.

In figure 5.11 consider a track size of three to illustrate

the sequential track allocation method. The file used is

{10, 6, 12, 5, 15, 9, 2, 13}.

The input sequence is from left to right.

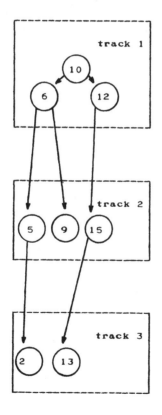

Figure 5.11. Sequential Binary tree Allocation.

In this allocation method the average number of track transitions in a search is 15/8.

5.2.2.   Retrieval Time

Muntz and Uzgalis [50] presented an approximate average number of references for a binary search tree stored sequentially on a direct access storage device. This average involved the assumption that after the first two tracks each node that is interrogated in a search path requires a new track reference. A new approximation to the number of references to the direct access storage device during a retrieval operation is presented. This approximation is developed without any assumptions about the first two tracks of the binary search tree.

Consider a tree stored in d buckets with size b. Let the number of keys in the tree be N. The number of buckets needed to store the tree is

$$k \; = \; \left\lceil \frac{N}{b} \right\rceil \; ,$$

where $\left\lceil \frac{N}{b} \right\rceil$ is the smallest integer not exceeded by $\frac{N}{b}$.

The tree is stored sequentially in the k buckets using the function $f(x)$ and $f^{-1}(x)$ to generate addresses to other buckets for those nodes within buckets that reference nodes in other buckets. Assume the keys are equally likely to arrive. The tree is constructed dynamically as the keys are received. Therefore, the structure of the tree is determined by the order in which the keys arrive.

The average internal or external path length is the average path length to an internal or external node. In a binary search tree with N internal nodes, there are N! sequences in the tree. Hibbard

derived formulas for the average internal and external path lengths.
The internal path length for a binary search tree defined by Hibbard
[29] is

$$\bar{l}(N) = 1.4\log_2(N),$$

where N is the number of nodes in the tree and $\bar{l}(N)$ is the
average internal path length. The root has path length equal to one.
So, $\log_2 1$ is assigned the value approximately one by $1.4\log_2(1.64)$.

The N records are divided into k buckets. To access the N
records k buckets must be accessed. The average number of records
assigned to each bucket is $m = \alpha b$, where b is the bucket size and α
is the load factor. The number of buckets is represented as

$$k = \frac{\alpha N}{m}.$$

Therefore the mean number of accesses to the direct access
storage device during a retrieval is

$$\bar{C}_R(\alpha,b) = 1.4\log_2(\frac{\alpha N}{m} + .64).$$

5.2.3. Insertion Algorithm

Algorithm B'' (Insertion in a hash rooted symbol tree stored
on a direct access storage device.)

Assume that BUCKET is a large storage pool of disk tracks
pointed to by AVAIL. Define R$\Leftarrow$AVAIL to be the removal of a node
from the available storage pool and the final management of the AVAIL
pointer and underflow conditions. The roots of the trees are stored
in a link vector called PT. A key-to-address transformation h(K) is
used to transform the keys into bucket addresses. The functions

ANEXT, ENEXT, ADATA, INFO, CODE, ATAG and ETAG operate on nodes defined in the data structure pointed to by the link variables. A link variable P is used to move along the tree from the root. Q is a temporary link variable used to move along the subtrees of a tree and its initial value is the value of P. The function f maps the track addresses into main memory addresses. Define READ(P) to mean the reading of a track from the direct access storage device containing the address P, into an internal main memory buffer. Define WRITE(P) to mean the writing of a track on the direct access storage device that contain an address P.

CODE $\begin{cases} - & \text{indicates the end of the string.} \\ \\ + & \text{indefinite continuation indicator.} \end{cases}$

INFO   is the stored character.

ANEXT is the address of the next filial set.

ENEXT is the address of the sibling.

ADATA is the address of data.

PT   is the pointer to the tree for a particular letter.

CT   is the number of nodes in the list pointed to by PT.

ROV   is the upper limit on the number of nodes in a list pointed to by PT before a continuation indicator is inserted in the list.

c   is the length of a list before a continuation.

ATAG = $\begin{cases} 0 & \text{ANEXT is a disk address in another track.} \\ \\ 1 & \text{ANEXT is a pointer within the track.} \end{cases}$

$$\text{ETAG} = \begin{cases} 0 & \text{ENEXT is a disk address in another track.} \\ \\ 1 & \text{ENEXT is a pointer within the track.} \end{cases}$$

B''1. [Initialize.] GET C, $j \leftarrow 1$, $i \leftarrow h(C_1)$, $P \leftarrow PT(i)$,
        IF (P = 0) THEN go to B''9.
        ENDIF.
        $P \leftarrow READ(P)$, $P \leftarrow f(P)$.
B''2. [Compare characters.] IF ($C_j = \triangledown$)
                                        THEN go to B''6.
                                ENDIF.
        IF (CODE(P) = '+')
            THEN IF (ATAG(P) = 0)
                        THEN DO $P \leftarrow READ(ADATA(P))$,
                                    $P \leftarrow f(P)$ ENDDO.
                    ENDIF.
            ELSE $P \leftarrow f(ADATA(P))$.
        ENDIF.
        IF (C_j = INFO(P)) THEN go to B''7.
        ENDIF.
B''3. [Check for code.]
        IF (CODE(P) = '+')
            THEN IF (ATAG(P) = 0)
                        THEN DO $P \leftarrow READ(ADATA(P))$,
                                    $P \leftarrow f(P)$ ENDDO.
                    ENDIF.
            ELSE $P \leftarrow f(ADATA(P))$.
        ENDIF.
        IF (CODE(P) = '-') THEN go to B''5.
        ENDIF.
B''4. [Is it a sibling or a filial set node?]
        IF (ETAG(P) = 0)
            THEN DO $P \leftarrow READ(ENEXT(P))$, $P \leftarrow f(P)$
                    ENDDO.
            ELSE $P \leftarrow f(ENEXT(P))$.
        ENDIF.
        go to B''2.
B''5. [Find the next part.]
        IF (ETAG(P) = 0)
            THEN DO $Q \leftarrow READ(ENEXT(P))$,
                        IF ($Q \neq 0$)
                            THEN $Q \leftarrow f(Q)$
                        ENDIF.
                    ENDDO.
            ELSE $Q \leftarrow f(ENEXT(P))$.
        ENDIF.

```
              IF ( Q = 0 ∧ C_j = ∇  THEN  go to B′′8.
              ENDIF.
              P ← Q, go to B′′2.
B′′6.   [Last character.] R⇌AVAIL,
        CT(i)←CT(i) + 1,
        IF (CT(i) > ROV(i)) THEN  CON(i),
        ENDIF.
        CODE(f(R))←′-′,
        ADATA(f(R))←ADR,
        ANEXT(P)←R,
        P←f^{-1}(P),
        WRITE(P),
        STOP.
B′′7.   [Look at the next character.]
        IF (ATAG(P) = 0)
             THEN  DO Q ← READ(ANEXT(P)),
                       IF (Q ≠ 0)  THEN  Q ← f(Q)
                       ENDIF.
                   ENDDO.
             ELSE  Q ← f(ANEXT(P)).
        ENDIF.
        IF (Q = 0)  THEN  go to B′′5.
        ENDIF.
        P ← Q, j ← j + 1, go to B′′2.
B′′8.   [Characters found.] AR ← ADATA(P), terminate.
B′′9.   [Store characters.] R⇌AVAIL,
        CT(i)←CT(i) + 1,
        IF (CT(i) > ROV(i)) THEN  CON(i),
        ENDIF.
        INFO(f(R))←C_j, IF (P ≠ 0)  THEN  ANEXT(P)←R
                        ENDIF.
        PT(i)←R,
        j←j + 1, P←f(R),
        IF (C_j = ∇)  THEN  go to B′′6.
        ENDIF.
        go to B′′9.



    CON(i):  CODE(f(R))←+, ADATA(P)←R,

             P←f(R), ROV(i)←ROV(i) + c,

             CT(i)←CT(i) + 1, R⇌AVAIL.
```

5.2.4.   Insertion Time

    The number of comparisons needed to find a key is exactly one more than the number of comparisons that were needed when that key was inserted into the tree. Therefore, the average number of accesses to the direct access storage device during an insertion operation is

$$\bar{C}_I(\alpha,b) = \bar{C}_R(\alpha,b) + 1.$$

5.2.5.   Deletion Algorithm

Algorithm B''' (Deletion in a hash rooted symbol tree stored

                    on a direct access storage device.)

    Assume that BUCKET is a large storage pool of disk tracks pointed to by AVAIL. Define AVAIL$\Leftarrow$P to be the return of a node to the available storage pool and the final management of the AVAIL pointer and overflow conditions. The roots of the trees are stored in a link vector called PT. A key-to-address transformation h(K) is used to transform the keys into bucket addresses. The functions ANEXT, ENEXT, ADATA, INFO, CODE, ATAG and ETAG operate on nodes defined in the data structure pointed to by the link variables. A link variable P is used to move along the tree from the root. Q is a temporary link variable used to move along the subtrees of a tree and its initial value is the value of P. The function f maps the track addresses into main memory addresses. Define READ(P) to mean the reading of a track from the direct access storage device containing the address P, into an internal main memory buffer. Define WRITE(P) to mean the writing of a track on the direct access storage device that contains an address P.

$$
\text{CODE} \begin{cases} - & \text{indicates the end of the string.} \\ \\ + & \text{indefinite continuation indicator.} \end{cases}
$$

INFO is the stored character.

ANEXT is the address of the next filial set.

ENEXT is the address of the sibling.

ADATA is the address of data.

PT   is the pointer to the tree for a particular letter.

$$
\text{ATAG} = \begin{cases} 0 & \text{ANEXT is a disk address in another track.} \\ \\ 1 & \text{ANEXT is a pointer within the track.} \end{cases}
$$

$$
\text{ETAG} = \begin{cases} 0 & \text{ENEXT is a disk address in another track.} \\ \\ 1 & \text{ENEXT is a pointer within the track.} \end{cases}
$$

B'''1. [Initialize.] GET C, $j \leftarrow 1$, $i \leftarrow h(C_1)$, $P \leftarrow PT(i)$.
        IF $(P = 0)$ THEN DO PUT "not found", STOP ENDDO.
        ENDIF.
        $P \leftarrow READ(P)$, $P \leftarrow f(P)$.
B'''2. [Compare characters.] IF $(C_j = \triangledown)$
                                        THEN go to B'''6.
                            ENDIF.
        IF $(CODE(P) = '+')$
            THEN IF $(ATAG(P) = 0)$
                    THEN DO $P \leftarrow READ(ADATA(P))$,

```
                                      P ← f( P ) ENDDO.
                           ENDIF.
                   ELSE    P ← f( ADATA( P ) ).
               ENDIF.
               IF ( C_j = INFO( P ) )  THEN   go to B'''7.
               ENDIF.
B'''3.   [Check for code.]
         IF ( CODE( P ) = '+' )
               THEN   IF ( ATAG( P ) = 0 )
                              THEN   DO P ← READ( ADATA( P ) ),
                                        P ← f( P ) ENDDO.
                      ENDIF.
                   ELSE   P ← f( ADATA( P ) ).
         ENDIF.
         IF ( CODE( P ) = '-' )  THEN   go to B'''5.
         ENDIF.
B'''4.   [Is it a sibling or a filial set node?]
         IF ( ETAG( P ) = 0 )
               THEN   DO P ← READ( ENEXT( P ) ), P ← f( P )
                      ENDDO.
                   ELSE   P ← f( ENEXT( P ) ).
         ENDIF.
         go to B'''2.




B'''5.   [Find the next part.]
         IF ( ETAG( P ) = 0 )
               THEN   DO Q ← READ( ENEXT( P ) ),
                         IF ( Q ≠ 0 )
                                 THEN   Q ← f( Q )
                         ENDIF.
                      ENDDO.
                   ELSE   Q ← f( ENEXT( P ) ).
         ENDIF.
         IF ( Q = 0 ∧ C_j = ∇ )  THEN   go to B'''8.
         ENDIF.
         P ← Q, go to B'''2.
B'''6.   [Last character.]
         IF ( CODE( P ) = '+' )
               THEN   IF ( ATAG( P ) = 0 )
                              THEN   DO P ← READ( ADATA( P ) ),
                                        P ← f( P ) ENDDO.
                      ENDIF.
                   ELSE   P ← f( ADATA( P ) ).
         ENDIF.
         IF ( CODE( P ) = '-' )  THEN   go to B'''8.
         ENDIF.
         PUT "not found", STOP.
B'''7.   [Look at the next character.]
         IF ( ATAG( P ) = 0 )
               THEN   DO Q ← READ( ANEXT( P ) ),
```

```
                    IF (Q ≠ 0)
                        THEN Q ← f(Q)
                    ENDIF.
                 ENDDO.
           ELSE   Q ← f(ANEXT(P)).
     ENDIF.
     IF (Q = 0) THEN  go to B′′′5.
     ENDIF.
     P ← Q, j ← j + 1, go to B′′′2.
B′′′8.  [Characters found.] CODE(P)←1, P←f⁻¹(P),
     WRITE(P), STOP.
```

5.2.6. Deletion Time

One may think that a long sequence of random deletions and insertions will degenerate the tree and thus invalidate the efficiency estimates. Hibbard has proved that after a random element is deleted from a random tree, the resulting tree is still random.

Assume that a deletion is made by inserting a deletion indicator in the node. This avoids processing the pointers to buckets in other tracks. At some later time the tree can be processed in a batch mode to remove the deleted nodes.

The average number of disk accesses to the direct access storage device is

$$\bar{C}_D(\alpha,b) = \bar{C}_R(\alpha,b).$$

5.2.7. Storage Space Requirements

Assume that each node of the buckets contain bits for the key and two links. The number of nodes required to store the tree on the direct access storage device is

$$\omega_s = \left\lceil \frac{N}{b} \right\rceil b,$$

where $\left\lceil \frac{N}{b} \right\rceil$ is the smallest integer not exceeded by $\frac{N}{b}$.

5.3.   Storing TRIE

5.3.1.   Retrieval Algorithm

A trie is defined in section 5.1. Figure 5.6 illustrates the nodes of a trie.

Storing a trie on a direct access device can be uneconomical. The M-place vectors with components corresponding to digits or characters require h accesses for a string of length h. The real advantage of this method is the addressing in the M-place vectors. Each node on level h represents the set of all keys that begin with a certain sequence of h characters. The node represented by the vector specifies an M-ary branch, depending on the (h + 1)st character.

One way to reduce the number of accesses to the direct access storage device is to use two characters at each level to index into the filial set pointers. This reduces the number of accesses by one half. In general, increasing the number of characters at each level by i, reduces the number of accesses to index into the filial set pointers by $\frac{h}{i}$.

Braindais pointed out that we can save memory space at the expense of running time if linked lists are used for each node vector of the trie. This is economical, since most entries in the vectors tend to be empty. This is equivalent to replacing a trie stored in a table by a forest of trees. The rooted tree in figure 5.9 generated by algorithm B is an illustration of a forest of trees rooted in ROOT.

5.3.2.   Retrieval Time

The average number of references to retrieve an item from a

trie stored on a direct access storage device has not been presented. In this section an average number of references to retrieve an item from a trie stored on a direct access storage device is presented.

Searching a trie for an item is done by levels. That is to say, the search proceeds from level to level starting from the root until the item is found. At each level h of the search a favorable conclusion depends on a favorable conclusion at level h - 1. So, an item with h characters or digits will require h levels to store it and h levels of search to locate it.

Assume that N symbol sequences or digits called keys are randomly chosen from the sequences possible in an n_e-valued alphabet. Suppose there are N keys in $\frac{N}{b}$ buckets. On level h there are $\frac{N}{b}$ buckets of nodes in the trie. The number of nodes on levels 1, 2, 3, ... is at least n_e, n_e^2, ...; hence

$$\frac{N}{b} \geq n_e^h \ .$$

Taking the n_e log of both sides of the expression above yields

$$h \leq \log_{n_e}(\frac{N}{b}) \ .$$

Define b = $\frac{m}{\alpha}$, where m is the average number of records in the buckets and α is the load factor. The average number of accesses to the direct access storage device is

$$\bar{C}_R(\alpha, m) \leq \log_{n_e}(\frac{\alpha N}{m}) \ .$$

5.3.3. Insertion Algorithm

Insertions in the trie are made using algorithm B´´ of section 5.2.3. The key is stored in the key vector C. The algorithm is executed starting at the first step. A return of found after termination indicates the key is in the file. When the key is not in the file it is inserted.

5.3.4. Insertion Time

An insertion is made by first initiating a retrieval. The number of comparisons needed to find a key is exactly one more than the number of comparisons that were needed when the key was inserted into the trie.

Therefore, the average number of accesses to the direct access storage device during an insertion operation is

$$\bar{C}_I(\alpha,b) = \bar{C}_R(\alpha,b) + 1.$$

5.3.5. Deletion Algorithm

Algorithm B''' of section 5.2.5 is used for deletions in the trie. The argument key is stored in the key vector C. The algorithm is executed starting at the first step. When the key is found, a deletion indicator is inserted and the algorithm terminates. A return of not found after termination indicates the key is not in the file.

5.3.6. Deletion Time

All items are deleted by first initiating a search. Since the trie is a forest, it can be represented by a tree. Any deletions from the trie generate another random tree.

The average number of accesses to the direct access storage device is

$$\bar{C}_D(\alpha,b) = \bar{C}_R(\alpha,b).$$

5.3.7. Storage Space Requirements

Since a trie can be represented as a forest of trees it can

be represented by a tree. A tree can be represented by a binary tree. It follows that our structure for storing a binary tree is adequate for storing a trie. The amount of storage required to store the trie is much more than that required for the tree, but it makes the processing of variable- length data easy.

Let n be the (average) number of elements possible in each key element position and x the average number of elements used in each position. The average number of nodes required to store the trie is given by Sussenguth [66] as

$$\omega_t = n \; \frac{x^h - 1}{x - 1} \; .$$

5.4. Summary

A data structure has been defined to store trees and tries on a direct access storage device. It has been used to show how an internal tree searching algorithm can be modified to search trees on a direct access storage device. This data structure is simple and easier to manage than the B-tree and B*-tree structures.

The approximation introduced to calculate the number of accesses using binary search trees is close to the simulation results presented by Muntz and Uzgalis [50]. Muntz and Uzgalis assumed that after the first two pages each path requires a new page reference. This assumption is not used in the method presented in this monograph. For this reason the simulation results are lower than the calculated results of the new method. Figure 5.12 illustrates the new binary search tree results and compares them to those of Muntz and Uzgalis simulations.

The average number of accesses have been calculated for a trie stored on a direct access device to locate a symbol sequence.

The performance measures calculated show that the method is efficient. Any efficiency desired is controlled by the user and the constraints of the direct access storage device.

Scidmore and Weinberg [62] calculated the mean search time for a trie stored as a linked structure in main memory. Modifying this method to store the list on a direct access storage device gives reasonable average search times. The method introduced in this chapter for the trie gives a more realistic average search time than the modified Scidmore and Weinberg method.

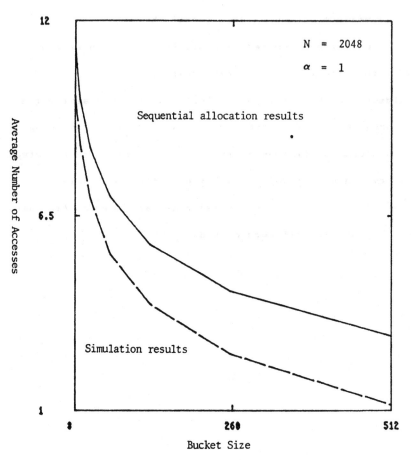

Figure 5.12.   Comparison of Sequential Allocation and
                Simulation Results

CHAPTER 6

RECORD_PROCESSING_USING_LINKED_FILES

In a retrieval, a set of records to which access is desired
is normally specified as a function of key words that identify the
various records. The retrieval operation consists of identifying the
addresses on the direct access storage device, which identifies those
records which are characterized by a given key.

Linked list structures are used to provide the necessary
associations between records. In these structures, pointers which
link each key word of a given record to the next record exhibiting
the same key words are used.

A directory, that contains for each available key word K_i,
an indicator giving the number of different lists pertaining to that
key word, is used. Included with each key word is the beginning
address of the corresponding list. In this arrangement, the search
process consists of a directory search on the direct access storage
device to identify the beginning addresses of the lists of records
containing the specified key words. After the list addresses are
identified, the direct access storage device is searched to identifiy
all records included in the lists.

In the limit, as many lists may exist for each key word as

there are records associated with that key. The length of the list
in this case is 1, and the number of entries in the directory equals
the product of the number of key words and the number of records per
word. In our case, the number of entries in the directory equals the
number of key words, and the length of each list is equal to the
number of records per key word. Whenever the length of each list of
records in the main file exceeds b, the bucket capacity, a new bucket
is linked to the current bucket.

6.1.   Storing_Linked_List_Files

A directory, with pointers to the list of records
associated with each key, is used to store the keys. This
arrangement separates the stored records into sets in such a way that
all records within a given set are identified by a common key word or
key word set.

Every record corresponds to one node on a list. If a
record is characterized by several directory key words, the record is
represented by a node that is at the intersection of the list
corresponding to the several key words. Figure 6.1 illustrates
schematically the structure of three records.

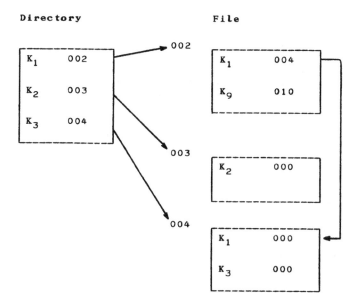

Directory   File

Figure 6.1.   Linked List File Organization.

6.1.1.   Retrieval Algorithm

Algorithm C´ (Retrieval using linear probing and

chaining with separate lists.)

The operators and variables have the same meaning as those

in section 4.2.1 for processing the record list.   The node structure

for the linear probing directory search is

INFO[i] is the record key.

LINK   is a pointer to the list of records.
[Find the key in the directory.]
Execute algorithm A´ in section 4.4.1.
i←LINK(i).
[Process the list of records.]
i←READ(i), i←f(i).

```
            DO
[Output record.]
            K←INFO[ i ].
[Advance to the next record.]
            IF (TAG( i ) ▪ 1)
                    THEN  DO i←LINK( i ), i←READ( i ),
                                i←f( i ) ENDDO.
                    ELSE  i←f( LINK( i ))
            ENDIF.
[Check for the end of the list.]
            IF ( i ▪ 0) THEN  STOP.
            ENDIF.
        ENDDO.
```

6.1.2.   Retrieval Time

Assume that the directory search is done by Linear Probing.
The contribution to the total retrieval time for the directory search
given in section 4.4.1 is

$$\bar{C}_R^*(\alpha,b) = 1 + t_b(\alpha) + t_{2b}(\alpha) + t_{3b}(\alpha) + \cdots ,$$

where

$$t_{nb}(\alpha) = \frac{\sum_{k \ge nb}^{\infty} (k - nb)P(k)}{\alpha nb} .$$

After a key word is located the address of the list is used to
retrieve the record.

Each record may occupy more than one bucket. Therefore,
more than one access to the direct access storage device is required
for nodes represented by long records. The address of the list in
the directory is a home address associated with the list. Assume
that the records are placed in the file according to a uniform random
distribution.

The lists (pointed to from the directory) are separate for
each key word. The average number of accesses in a search of the
list defined in section 4.2.2 is

$$\bar{C}_R^{**}(\alpha,b) = 1 + \frac{1}{2m} \sum_{k > b}^{N} (k^2 - 2kb + k + b^2 - b)\frac{(\alpha b)^k}{k!} e^{-\alpha b} .$$

The average number of accesses to the direct access storage device while searching a linked list file is

$$\bar{C}_R(\alpha,b) = \bar{C}_R^*(\alpha,b) + \bar{C}_R^{**}(\alpha,b) .$$

6.1.3.   Insertion Algorithm

Algorithm C'' (Insertion using linear probing and

chaining with separate lists.)

The operators and variables have the same meaning as those in section 4.2.3 for inserting a record in a list.   The node structure for the linear probe directory search is

```
 _____
|     |     |
|     |     |
|INFO |LINK |
|     |     |
|_____|_____|
```

[Insert the key into the directory.]
        Execute algorithm A'' in section 4.4.3.
        $Q \leftarrow i$.
        DO
[Read the file containing the records and
 remove the key.]
        $K^* \leftarrow$ INFO(f((READ(P)))
        IF (end of records)   THEN   DO WRITE($f^{-1}(Q)$),
                                      STOP ENDDO.
        ENDIF.
[Compare the key to the record key.]
        IF ($K = K^*$)
                THEN   DO
[The keys are the same.]
                      IF (HEAD(i) = 0)
                          THEN   DO TAG(Q)$\leftarrow$1,
                                  TAG(P)$\leftarrow$1
                                  ENDDO.
                          ELSE   NODE(HEAD(i))$\leftarrow$
                                  NODE(HEAD(i)) - 1.
                    ENDIF.
                    LINK(Q)$\leftarrow$P,
                    WRITE($f^{-1}(Q)$),
                    Q$\leftarrow$f(P)
                ENDDO.
        ENDIF.
        ENDDO.

6.1.4.   Insertion Time

A search is made of the directory for the key word. If the key word is not in the directory, it is inserted in the directory and a list is created for records associated with the key word. If the key word is in the directory no action is taken.

The average number of accesses to the direct access storage device in an insertion operation is

$$\bar{C}_I(\alpha,b) = \bar{C}_R^*(\alpha,b) + \sum_{k>b}^{\infty} (k - b) P(k).$$

6.1.5.   Deletion Algorithm

Algorithm C''' (Deletion using linear probing and

chaining with separate lists)

C'''1. [Find the key in the directory and insert a

deletion indicator.]

Execute algorithm A''' in section 4.4.5.

6.1.6.   Deletion Time

The directory is searched for the key word. If the key word is not located the process terminates. When the key word is located, it is replaced in the directory by a deletion indicator and the pointer to the list is set to zero.

The average number of accesses to the direct access storage device is

$$\bar{C}_D(\alpha,b) = \bar{C}_R^*(\alpha,b) + \sum_{k>b}^{\infty} (k - b) P(k).$$

6.1.7.   Storage Space Requirements

Space requirements include space for the directory and space for the linked list.

The total space requirement for the directory is

$$\omega_p = bd .$$

The total average space required by the linked lists is

$$\omega_c = bd + d \sum_{k>b}^{\infty} (k - b)P(k).$$

The total space required for linked list files, denoted by ω_f, is

$$\omega_f = \omega_p + \omega_c .$$

6.2. Storing Double Linked List Files

The only real advantage in storing files as double linked list files is the speed of traversing the list. The internal search algorithms for double linked lists are faster than those for linked list and circular linked lists. But, we are not concerned with internal search speeds.

Our files are very large. The file and its directory must be stored on a direct access storage device. The major factor considered is the number of accesses to the direct access storage device to process a request. Assume that the directory is accessed using Linear Probing. The number of accesses to the direct access storage device while retrieving, inserting, and deleting information is the same as that for the linked list file organization.

6.2.1. Storage Space Requirements

The total space required for the directory is

$$\omega_p = bd .$$

The file lists are stored as double linked lists. The average storage required for the file list is

$$\omega_{dl} = bd + d \sum_{k>b}^{\infty} (k - b)P(k).$$

Therefore, the total space required for double linked list files, denoted by ω_{ll} is

$$\omega_{ll} = \omega_p + \omega_{dl} \ .$$

The total average space required for this file is the same as that for the linked list files. A double linked list file has two pointers in each word. Hence, this file contain less space to store keys.

6.3.   Storing_Ring_List_Files

This structure uses circular linking in both the LLINK and RLINK directions. Assume that Linear Probing is used in the directory. The average number of accesses to the direct access storage device is the same as that for the linked list structure.

The storage requirement is the same as that for the double linked list structure.

CHAPTER 7

RECORD PROCESSING USING INVERTED FILES

In many cases, it is desired to organize the records of a data base to reflect data base characteristics and data base usage. The importance of these organizations becomes clear when one key is associated with more than one record and many keys are associated with the same record. Under these conditions, it is necessary to store the records in a structure that maximizes the use of the storage space occupied by the records on the direct access device and minimizes the time required to process the records.

Lowe [38] studied the influence of data base characteristics and usage on direct access file organization. In this study, he derived measures of performance for an _inverted file_ which is a file organization derived from the chained organization by decreasing the length of each chain to one and correspondingly increasing the directory size to include for each key word as many entries as there are records characterized by that key word. The analysis used a function to characterize the data base and a function to characterize the use of the data base. All measures are developed using these functions and combinations of the assumption of uniform distribution and a qualitative rank- probability relationship called Zipf's law.

A useful distribution presented in Knuth [34] is

$$p(j,\theta) = \frac{1}{j^{1-\theta}H(N,\theta)} \quad .$$

where,

$$H(N,\theta) = 1^{-(1-\theta)} + 2^{-(1-\theta)} + \ldots + N^{-(1-\theta)} \quad .$$

When $\theta = \dfrac{\log .80}{\log .20}$, it approximates the 80-20 rule.

When $\theta = 1$, $p(j,1)$ is a uniform distribution. For $\theta = 0$, $p(j,0)$ is Zipfian or it obeys Zipf's law, introduced by Zipf [71]. We have

$$p(j,0) = \frac{1}{j\sum\limits_{k=1}^{N}\frac{1}{k}} \quad .$$

For N large

$$\sum\limits_{k=1}^{N}\frac{1}{k} = \ln N + \gamma,$$

where γ is Euler's constant and is approximately

$$\gamma = 0.5772.$$

The form of Zipf probability is approximated by

$$p(j,0) = \frac{1}{j(\ln N + \gamma)} \quad ,$$

for $N > 100$.

Summaries on organization of data as inverted files are presented in [10, 20, 30, 57, 60].

In this monograph the load time, retrieval time, update time, and memory utilization are investigated for direct access inverted files. An inverted file is illustrated in figure 7.1.

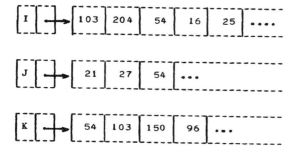

a. Inverted List Structure

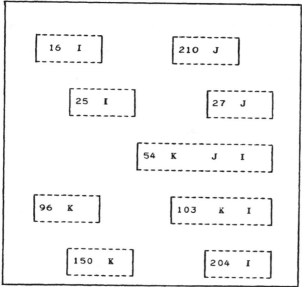

b. Main File

Figure 7.1.   Inverted File Structure.

7.1.   Generation Of Inverted File

In this section the inverted file is analyzed. Any analysis of an inverted file must include those factors that are related to the basic use of the file. The basic factors related to the use of inverted files are file loading, retrieving items from the file, file update and storage space requirements. File update consists of file operations involving inserting and deleting items.

The time required to load an inverted file is called load time. This process involves actually inverting the file if an inverted copy is not available. For large files the inverting operation requires a large amount of computer time.

From time to time information is deleted and inserted into the file. The time spent deleting and inserting information is called the update time. In this process records are changed one-by-one on demand. Generally, updating the inverted file is an expensive operation.

Storage space is a critical factor that must be considered when using an inverted file. This is critical because the original file and the inverted file must be kept on the direct access storage device.

Algorithm C is presented to quantify the work done while inverting a file with the file and the inverted file stored on a direct access storage device.

Algorithm C (Inverted File)

Define L to be a link variable whose content is the address of the first item of a particular record in the file to be inverted. The pointer H points to the first record of the file to be inverted.

Define READ H s as an operation that reads the record at H into

buffer s and increments H in such a way that H points to the next

record to be read.

A frequency function $g(j)$ is used to collect a count of the

occurrence of items in the file. The file is inverted on every item

in the file to allow retrieval of any item. AVAIL is a stack of

allocated record slots. The operation $R \leftrightarrows$ AVAIL is the popping

of the stack and the final management of the stack pointers. When

the algorithm terminates, the inverted file and its structure are on

the direct access storage device pointed to by V.

The auxillary variables used in this algorithm are c, i, j,

k, r, z, l, M, w_j, q_j, and $I_{j,k}$. Define the operation variable

$\leftrightarrows 0$ to mean the initialization of every position of storage

defined by the variable to zero. The variable l is an upper bound on

the number of pointers allowed in a buffer. The variables c, i, j,

and k are indices controlled by the algorithm. The bounds on these

indices are:

$$1 \leq i \leq l; \quad 1 \leq j \leq M; \quad 4 \leq k \leq l,$$

where M is the number of buffers. A three value switch r is used as

a control in the algorithm. The w vector indicates the state of the

buffers. When a buffer is first updated the associated w is set to

one. Before releasing any buffer its associated w is checked. An

associated w value of one will cause the buffer location to be

written on the direct access storage device and w is set to zero. A

link variable P and a link vector q_j are used to control the

pointers, which are direct access storage device addresses during a

READ and a WRITE.

The ITEM function has the property that it locates the next item in the bucket. After locating the item, the index is incremented to the position in the bucket under the last character of the current item.

A buffer area called $I_{j,k}$ is used to store item names and pointers. The $I_{j,k}$ indicates the jth item name buffer in main memory and the kth location within the item name buffer. To insert a pointer in a given item, name buffer k must be incremented first, then the insertion is made.

The data structure used in algorithm C is illustrated in figure 7.2.

item	g(j)	k	pointer to next item name	pointers to master file	pointer to next record of current item name

a.   Node Structure

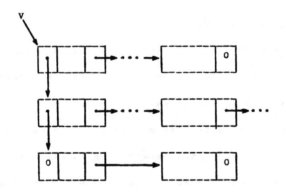

Figure 7.2.   Inverted File.

C1. [Initialization.] $j \leftarrow 1$, $w_j \leftarrow 0$, $q_j \stackrel{\leftarrow}{=} 0$,

$I_{j,k} \stackrel{\leftarrow}{=} 0$, $r \leftarrow 0$, $D \leftarrow V$.

C2. [Read a record of the file to be inverted.]
$i \leftarrow 1$, $c \leftarrow i$, $L \leftarrow H$, READ H s, $z \leftarrow ITEM(s_c)$.

C3. [Has the last record been processed?]
IF (H = 0) THEN DO $j \leftarrow 1$, go to C10 ENDDO.
ENDIF.

C4. [Last record has not been processed. Is there an
inverted file record?]
IF (D = 0) THEN go to C13.
ENDIF.
$q_j \leftarrow D$, READ D I_j.

C5. [Is the item in the buffer?]
IF ($I_{j,1} \neq z$) THEN go to C15.
ENDIF.

C6. [The item is in the buffer. Has the buffer been
updated?] IF (w_j = 0) THEN $w_j \leftarrow 1$.
ENDIF.

C7. [Is the buffer for this item full ?] $k \leftarrow I_{j,3}$,
IF (k + 1 > l) THEN go to C14.
ENDIF.

C8. [The buffer is not full. Update buffer.]
$g(I_{j,2}) \leftarrow g(I_{j,2}) + 1$, $I_{j,k+1} \leftarrow L + i$,
$I_{j,3} \leftarrow k + 1$, $i \leftarrow c$, $z \leftarrow ITEM(s_c)$.

C9. [End of J buffer?]
IF (c > l)
THEN DO $j \leftarrow 1$, $r \leftarrow 2$, go to C10 ENDDO.
ENDIF.
go to C6.

C10. [Write all updated buffers on direct access
storage device.]
IF (w_j = 1)
THEN DO WRITE q_j I_j, $w_j \leftarrow 0$ ENDDO.
ENDIF.
$j \leftarrow j + 1$.

C11. [Have all buffers been written?]
IF (J > M) THEN go to C12.
ENDIF.
go to C10.

C12. [Terminate if all records have been inverted.]
IF (r = 2)
THEN go to C1.
ELSE IF (r = 0)
THEN STOP.
ENDIF.
ENDIF.

C13. [Allocate a new buffer for this item.]
$R \stackrel{\leftarrow}{=} AVAIL$,

```
        IF ( r = 1 )
                THEN   DO I_{j-1,4} ← R,   WRITE q_{j-1}   I_{j-1}
                       ENDDO.
        ENDIF.
        j←1,   q_j ← R,   I_{j,1} ← z,   I_{j,2} ← 0,
        I_{j,3} ← 4,   i←0,   r←0,
        IF ( V = 0 )
                THEN   DO D←R,   V←D ENDDO.
        ENDIF.
        w_j ← 1,  go to C5.
C14.  [Process chain for this item to find an empty
       position.] P←I_{j,k+1}.
        IF ( P = 0 )
                THEN   DO R ⇐ AVAIL,   I_{j,k+1} ← R,
                          WRITE q_j   I_j.   w_j ← 0,   q_j ← R,
                          I_{j,3} ← 4,   k←4,   go to C8
                       ENDDO.
                ELSE   IF ( w_j = 1 )
                          THEN   DO WRITE q_j   I_j.
                                    w_j ← 0 ENDDO.
                       ENDIF.
        ENDIF.
        READ P  I_j,   q_j ← P,  go to C7.
C15.  [The item is not in this buffer. Check all buffers
       in main memory.] j←j + 1,
        IF ( j ≤ M )  THEN   go to C5.
        ENDIF.
        IF ( w_{j-1} = 1 )
                THEN   DO WRITE q_{j-1}   I_{j-1},
                          w_{j-1} ← 0 ENDDO.
        ENDIF.
        q_{j-1} ← D,   READ D  I_{j-1}.
        IF ( D = 0 )  THEN   DO r←1,  go to C10 ENDDO.
        ENDIF.
        j←j - 1,   go to C5.
```

7.2. Load Time

When the inverted file exists, the load time is the amount
of time required to ready the direct access storage device for
accessing. Assume that the existence of the inverted file implies
the files readiness for accessing at any time with small delays that

are negligible. Under these assumptions, the load time is that time required to invert the file.

Assume that the items are randomly distributed in the file J to be inverted. The file J is read record-by-record until an end of file is encountered. Assume there are F records in J with length η. Each READ of J produces one buffer s full of information, which is the size of one record. Assume there always exists direct access storage space to hold the inverted file.

Define a_s to be the access time of the direct access storage device. The total time spent accessing J, denoted by A_J, is

$$A_J = a_s F.$$

Algorithm C reads a buffer s full of information and a sequential scan on an item-by-item basis is used to locate the items in s. Assume, for simplicity, that the items are of fixed length in J. To be more precise, let the length of each item be one unit. Therefore, the total units of scan time A_s for a buffer is

$$A_s = \eta.$$

Assume an equal probability of assigning an item to any of the available buckets d with a capacity of b items each. That is, restrict M in algorithm C to one. This forces algorithm C to access the direct access storage device for the inverted file V on every distinct nonadjacent item in s. Every access of V requires a write. So, the number of accesses equals the number of writes.

The load factor is

$$\alpha = \frac{m}{b},$$

where

$$m = \frac{nF}{d} \quad \text{and} \quad N = \eta F.$$

Let X be the random variable that is Poisson with parameter m,

$$P(X = k) = P(k) = \frac{m^k e^{-m}}{k!} \quad .$$

This is the probability that k items are assigned to a bucket.

All items, assigned to a bucket associated with a particular item name in excess of its capacity, are assigned to other buckets linked to the first bucket associated with the item name.

To quantify the mean number of items in the buckets, consider a counting process in continuous time. The events occur in the interval $[0, t]$. Consider the events

$$A_t = x \qquad \text{or less counts in } [0, t]$$

$$B_t = x + 1 \quad \text{or more counts in } [0, t].$$

Then we have

$$A_t \cup B_t = S_t, \quad A_t \cap B_t = \emptyset.$$

This implies that

$$P(A_t) + P(B_t) = 1.$$

The waiting time for $x + 1$ counts is less than or equal to t, for $x + 1$ or more counts in $[0, t]$.

Let $G_t(x) = P(X(t) \leq x)$,

$$F_{x+1}(t) = P(T(x+1) \leq t)$$

Then

$$G_t(x) = P(A_t) \quad \text{and} \quad F_{x+1}(t) = P(B_t).$$

So,

$$G_t(x) + F_{x+1}(t) = 1 \qquad\qquad (7.1)$$

The Poisson case with $t = m$ yields

$$\sum_{k=0}^{x} \frac{m^k e^{-m}}{k!} + \frac{1}{\Gamma(x+1)} \int_0^m u^x e^{-u} du = 1.$$

But

$$\sum_{k=0}^{x} p(k;m) + \sum_{k=x+1}^{\infty} p(k;m) = 1.$$

This yields

$$\sum_{k=x+1}^{\infty} p(k;m) = \frac{1}{\Gamma(x+1)} \int_0^m u^x e^{-u} du. \qquad (7.2)$$

Let the number of items in the ith bucket be Z_i.

$$P(Z_1 = k) = P(X = k); \quad k = 0, \ldots, b_1 - 1.$$

$$P(Z_1 = b_1) = P(X \geq b_1).$$

Since X is Poisson with parameter m,

$$P(Z_1 = k) = \frac{m^k e^{-m}}{k!}; \quad k = 0, \ldots, b_1 - 1$$

$$P(Z_1 = b_1) = \sum_{k=b_1}^{\infty} \frac{m^k e^{-m}}{k!}.$$

From (7.2) we have

$$P(Z_1 = b_1) = \frac{1}{\Gamma(b_1)} \int_0^m u^{b_1-1} e^{-u} du.$$

This is an incomplete Gamma function. Therefore, the expected number of items in the bucket is

$$E(Z_1) = \sum_{k=0}^{b_1-1} k \frac{m^k e^{-m}}{k!} + \frac{b_1}{\Gamma(b_1)} \int_0^m u^{b_1-1} e^{-u} du.$$

Define $\bar{O}(m,Z_1) = E(Z_1)$.

In the two bucket problem, let b_i be the number of places in bucket one and two for $i = 1, 2$ respectively. The number of items assigned to the last bucket is y, with random variable Y_1. The mean number of items assigned to a bucket in this problem is

$$P(X \leq b) = P(X^* = b) = P(Y_l = 0),$$

$$P(X = b + y) = P(X^* = b + y) = P(Y_l = y),$$

where

$$y = 1, 2, 3, \ldots \infty \quad \text{and} \quad X^* - b = Y_l.$$

$$Z_1 = k, \quad \text{if} \quad k = 0, 1, 2, \ldots b_1$$

$$Z_1 = b_1, \quad \text{if} \quad k = b_1, b_1 + 1, \ldots \infty.$$

$$\overline{O}(m, Z_1) = \sum_{k=0}^{b_1} kP(X = k) + b_1 \sum_{k=b_1+1}^{\infty} P(X = k),$$

$$\overline{O}(m, Z_1) = \sum_{k=1}^{b_1-1} kP(X = k) + \frac{b_1 \Gamma_m(b_1)}{\Gamma(b_1)}.$$

The average number of items in the last bucket is

$$\overline{O}(m, Y_l) = \overline{O}(m, X^*) - b.$$

In a three bucket problem we have,

$$P(X \leq b_1 + b_2) = P(X^* = b_1 + b_2) = P(Y_l = 0),$$

$$P(X = b_1 + b_2 + y) = P(X^* = b_1 + b_2 + y) = P(Y_l = y),$$

where

$$y = 1, 2, 3, \ldots \infty \quad \text{and} \quad X^* - b_1 - b_2 = Y_l.$$

The average number of items in the buckets are

$$\overline{O}(m, Z_1 + Z_2) = \sum_{k=1}^{b_1+b_2-1} kP(X = k) + (b_1 + b_2) \sum_{k=b_1+b_2}^{\infty} P(X=k),$$

$$\overline{O}(m, Z_1 + Z_2) = \sum_{k=1}^{b_1+b_2-1} kP(X = k) + (b_1 + b_2) \frac{\Gamma_m(b_1 + b_2)}{\Gamma(b_1 + b_2)}.$$

The average number of items in the first bucket has not changed.

Therefore, the average number of items in the second bucket is

$$\bar{O}(m, Z_2) = \bar{O}(m, Z_1 + Z_2) - \bar{O}(m, Z_1).$$

The average number of items in the last bucket is

$$\bar{O}(m, Y_l) = \bar{O}(m, X^*) - (b_1 + b_2).$$

In general, for a d bucket problem we have

$$\bar{O}(m, b) = \sum_{k=1}^{bd-1} kP(X = k) + bd \sum_{k=bd}^{\infty} p(X = k),$$

$$\bar{O}(m, b) = \sum_{k=1}^{bd-1} kP(X = k) + bd \frac{\Gamma_m(bd)}{\Gamma(bd)}.$$

Since the keys are identically distributed, the average number of buckets is $\frac{d}{\eta F}$. A sequential scan is used in algorithm C to locate an item name list on the direct access storage device. This scan length requires, on the average,

$$A_g = \left(\frac{j + 1}{2}\right) , \quad j = 1, 2, \ldots, \eta F,$$

accesses to find the item name during a file load. The average number of accesses to store the entire collection of items is

$$\bar{L}_t(m, b) = N(2 + \frac{2d}{\eta F} \bar{O}(m, b) + A_g).$$

7.3. Retrieval Algorithm

An item name located in s is searched for in an inverted file pointed to by V. Algorithm D determines if an item name is in the inverted file. After a favorable determination is made, the items associated with the item name are returned. An unfavorable determination results in an algorithm termination, indicating the item is not found.

Algorithm D (Retrieval From An Inverted File)

Define a function OUTPUT   s to output the information

pointed to by $I_{j,i}$ in s.

D1. [Initialization.] $j \leftarrow 1$, $D \leftarrow V$, $i \leftarrow 0$, $z \leftarrow ITEM(s_i)$.

D2. [Read an inverted file name record.] READ D I_j.

D3. [Is this the last name record?]
IF (D = 0) THEN DO PUT "not found", STOP ENDDO.
ENDIF.

D4. [Is this the item name?]
IF ($I_{j,1} \neq z$) THEN go to D2.
ENDIF.

D5. [The item name has been found.] $k \leftarrow I_{j,3}$, $i \leftarrow k$.

D6. [Have all the item name pointers been processed?]
IF (i = 0) THEN go to D8.
ENDIF.

D7. [All item name pointers have not been processed.
Read file to obtain the information pointed to by
the item name pointer.] $P \leftarrow I_{j,i}$, READ P s,
OUTPUT s, $i \leftarrow i - 1$, go to D6.

D8. [Is there another bucket of item name pointers?]
IF ($I_{j,k+1} = 0$) THEN DO PUT "finished",
STOP ENDDO.
ENDIF.

D9. [Get another bucket of item name pointers.]
$D \leftarrow I_{j,k+1}$, READ D I_j, go to D5.

7.4. Retrieval Time

Assume that the number of probes required to address

all items in an inverted list is

$$t_k = k + \frac{k - b}{2} ,$$

where $k > b$.

The inverted file directory should be organized to reduce the list

length. This leads to the optimistic assumption about the inverted

list in this section. Assume the average number of times the main

file is accessed is the same as the average number of probes per

record addressed. The expected value of the number of probes per

item addressed is the mean number of probes per list divided by the

mean number of items per list. This yields

$$\bar{C}_R(\alpha,b) = 2\left(\frac{\sum\limits_{k=0}^{N} t_k P(k)}{\sum\limits_{k=0}^{N} kP(k)}\right) \cdot$$

The average number of accesses including the directory search is

$$\bar{C}_R(\alpha,b) = 2 + \frac{1}{m}\sum\limits_{k>b}^{N}(k-b)P(k) + A_g.$$

For Zipf's law and the uniform distribution we have

$$\bar{C}_R(\alpha,b) = 2\left(\frac{\sum\limits_{k=0}^{N} t_k p(k,\theta)}{\sum\limits_{k=0}^{N} kp(k,\theta)}\right) + A_g \cdot$$

The assumption that the keys are distributed Poisson, Uniform, or Zipf in the buckets is essentially the same. This is illustrated in figure 7.3 for $A_g = 0$.

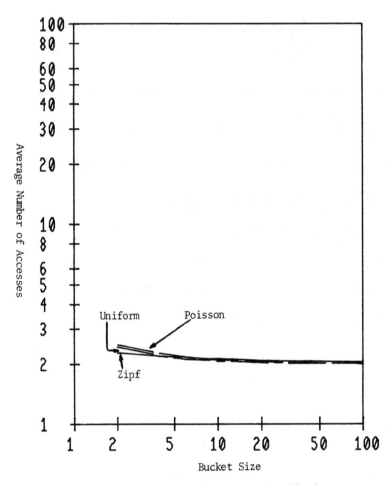

Figure 7.3. Retrieval Inverted File Distributions

Load Factor $\alpha = 1$

7.5. Insertion Algorithm

Assume that any item name inserted is first appended to file J. In algorithm C initialize $H \leftarrow 0$, L to point to the record appended to the file to be inverted, $w_j \stackrel{\pm}{=} 0$, $q_j \stackrel{\pm}{=} 0$, $M \leftarrow 1$, $D \leftarrow V$, $r \leftarrow 0$, $c \leftarrow i$, and $Z \leftarrow ITEM(s_c)$. Start algorithm C at step C4 to perform the insertion.

7.6. Insertion Time

One access is required to append the new item to file J. The average number of accesses in an insertion is

$$\bar{C}_I(m,b) = 2 + \frac{2d}{\eta F} \bar{O}(m,b) + A_g.$$

Clearly, the insertion time will be less if the directory search is binary. In this case

$$A_g = \log_2(N).$$

7.7. Deletion Algorithm

Algorithm E is used to delete an item name from the inverted file. Define a function BLANK that replaces the content of an item pointer by blanks.

Algorithm E (Deleting From An Inverted File)

  E1. [Initialization.] $j \leftarrow 1$, $D \leftarrow V$, $i \leftarrow 0$, $T \leftarrow D$, $z \leftarrow ITEM(s_i)$.

  E2. [Read an inverted file name record.] $U \leftarrow D$, READ D I_j.

  E3. [Is this the last name record?]
IF (D = 0) THEN   DO PUT "not found", STOP ENDDO.
ENDIF.

  E4. [Is this the item name?]
IF ($I_{j,1} \neq z$)
      THEN DO $U \leftarrow T$, go to E2 ENDDO.
      ELSE $S \leftarrow U$.
ENDIF.

  E5. [The item name has been found.] $k \leftarrow I_{j,3}$, $i \leftarrow k$.

  E6. [Have all item name pointers been processed?]
IF (i = 0)

THEN   DO AVAIL $\rightleftharpoons$ S,   go to E8 ENDDO.

ENDIF.

E7.   [All item name pointers have not been processed.
Read file to obtain the information pointed to by
the item name pointer.] P←$I_{j,i}$,   READ P s,

BLANK s,   WRITE $I_{j,i}$ s,   i←i - 1,   go to E6).

E8.   [Is there another bucket of item name pointers?]
IF ($I_{j,k+1}$ = 0)

      THEN   IF (D = 0)

            THEN   DO S←U,   READ S   s,
                        s←0,   WRITE U   s,
                        PUT "finished" ENDDO.

        ENDIF.

      ELSE   DO S←T,   READ S s, s_4←D,

          WRITE T s,   PUT "finished"
          ENDDO.

ENDIF.

E9.   [Get another bucket of item name pointers.]
E←$I_{j,k+1}$,   S←E,   READ E I_j,   go to E5.

7.8.   Deletion Time

The average number of accesses in the deletion process is

$$\bar{C}_D(m,b) = 1 + \frac{2d}{\eta \bar{F}} \bar{O}(m,b) + A_g.$$

7.9.   Storage Space Requirements

Let the total number of distinct items used to characterize
the entire data base be σ.   Number the distinct item names in such a
way that every item name is identified by a unique number $1 \leq j \leq \sigma$,
and the rank of the jth item name is j.

If g(j) is the total number of times that the item name
numbered j is used in characterizing all the items in the file, then
g(j) items are characterized by the jth item name.

A record of the inverted file may extend over more than one
bucket, in which case, more than one bucket is needed to store the
record.   The process of placing more than one short record in one
bucket is called packing.   When records are packed the portion of the
bucket unused is wasted.

Define n as the number of units of direct access storage required to store one item. The minimum memory requirement is

$$n\sum_{j=1}^{\sigma} g(j).$$

Let S_s be the total memory required for storage of the inverted files, including wasted memory. A bucket capacity of b yields

$$S_s(n,b) = nb \left\{ \sum_{j=1}^{\sigma} \left\lceil \frac{g(j)}{b} \right\rceil \right\} + \eta F.$$

where $\left\lceil \frac{g(j)}{b} \right\rceil$ is the smallest integer greater than or equal to $\frac{g(j)}{b}$.

7.10.   Summary

The inverted file has been generated essentially by using the chain organization with the length of each chain equal to one item. This increased the directory size to include, for each key, as many entries as there are items characterized by that key.

The search time is shortened by eliminating all pointers from the main file and performing most of the search in the directory. The directory search is linear in all derivations. However, other directory organizations may be used by defining A_g as the average search length for the organization.

Update time is consistent with our knowledge about updating inverted files. This is a tedious task because the accession list in the directory are maintained in a specific order.

In this analysis, M in algorithm C has been set to one. Many interesting cases develop when M is some positive value greater than one. An entire class of buffer management problems with interesting analysis occurs. These problems are not analyzed in this monograph.

CHAPTER 8

COMPARISON OF METHODS

8.1. Criterion For Comparison

Consider a very large data base that consists of 10 million records, 1000 words each, with an average of 15 keywords per record.

In comparing very large data bases, it is very difficult to summarize in a few words all revelant details of the "tradeoffs" involved in the choice of a data structure and a search method. The object of primary importance, with respect to speed of searching and the requisite storage space, is the average number of accesses to the direct access storage device during a search.

Graphs are used in the comparisons to display the relationships between load factor, the number of accesses, and the bucket size for various data structures and search methods. The effects of various combinations of search methods are also presented to find the point where one method should be discontinued and another method used.

The parameters are summarized and placed in an attribute list. All method names are defined in terms of meaningful symbols to generate a comparison criterion.

Summary of parameters in the attribute list are:

1. N - number of uniquely identified records to

   be stored.

2. d - number of buckets in the primary storage area.

3. b - bucket size in words.

4. bd - number of records in the primary storage area.

5. α - primary storage loading factor.

The operation list is:

1. R - retrieval.

2. I - insertion.

3. D - deletion.

The name list is:

1. CS - chaining with separate lists.

2. CC - chaining with coalescing lists.

3. LP - linear probing.

4. BS - binary search trees.

5. T - trie.

6. IF - inverted file.

7. LL - linked list.

8. DL - double linked list.

9. RL - ring list.

The distribution list is

1.   - Poisson

2. ϵ - 80-20 rule

3. z - Zipf's law

4. μ - Uniform

The result list is:

1. $\bar{C}_\delta$ — average number of accesses, where δ is an element of the operation list.

2. $\bar{\nu}$ — mean overflow.

3. $r_p = \dfrac{\bar{\nu}}{m}$ — percentage overflow.

4. $\rho = \dfrac{(m - \bar{\nu})}{b}$ — utilization of primary area.

A comparison of methods is defined as

$\bar{F}$(name list element/distribution, operation list element, attribute list elements).

An example of a comparison of the retrieval time of chaining with separate lists and chaining with coalescing lists is

$\bar{F}(CS:CC, R, (N,d,\alpha))$.

8.2.   Comparison

8.2.1.   Load Time

The average load time for the inverted file is defined in section 7.2 as $\bar{L}_t(\alpha,b)$.

The average load time for binary search trees is the total number of insertions incurred while building the the tree structure for the entire data base. Insertion time is defined in section 5.2.4 as $\bar{C}_I(\alpha,b)$. Assume there are N distinct keys to be loaded. The total load time is

$\bar{L}_t(\alpha,b) = N\bar{C}_I(\alpha,b)$.

The trie is loaded by an insertion operation.   Insertion

time for the trie is defined in 5.3.4 as $\bar{C}_I(\alpha,b)$. The total

load time for N distinct keys is

$$\bar{L}_t(b)=N\bar{C}_I(\alpha,b).$$

Loading linked files requires a directory search. The

total average load time for N distinct keys is

$$\bar{L}_t(\alpha,b) = N(\bar{C}_R^*(\alpha,b) + \bar{C}_R^{**}(\alpha,b)).$$

8.2.2.   Retrieval_Times

All files are assumed to be loaded when a request is made

to find an item.

A trie is stored as a symbol tree. An alphabet of ten

characters is used in the trie comparison.

The comparison is $\bar{F}$(CS:CC:LP:BS:T:IF:LL, R, (150000000,

d, 1)) and $\bar{F}$(CS:CC:LP:BS:T:IF:LL, R, (150000000, d, .5)).

The average number of accesses to the direct access

storage device is illustrated in figure 8.1 and figure 8.2 All

averages are generated as a function of the number of items in the

file and the number of available buckets.

A unique key assumption is used with every method but the

inverted file method.   The other methods must be adjusted for

identical keys in all comparisons.   The average number of identical

keys in an inverted file bucket is $\bar{O}(\alpha,b)$.   Assume that the

other methods are modified to retrieve, insert and delete identical

keys.   The adjustment for a comparison is the product of the average

number of accesses and $\bar{O}(\alpha,b)$.   A good approximation to

$\bar{O}(\alpha,b)$ is αb.

In figure 8.2, chaining with separate lists minimizes the number of accesses for bucket sizes less than 8. The trie minimum changes with x. Increasing x increases the mean number of accesses. This factor should be considered when selecting the trie.

The retrieval time may be reduced by applying the 80-20 rule. In most cases

$$\tilde{C}_R(\alpha,b,.2,.8) < \bar{C}_R(\alpha,b).$$

8.2.3. Insertion Time

The comparison is $\bar{F}$(CS:CC:LP:BS:T:IF:LL, I, (150000000, d, 1)) and $\bar{F}$(CS:CC:LP:BS:T:IF:LL, I, (150000000, d, .5)).

Figure 8.3 and figure 8.4 illustrate the relationships between various insertion methods. Again, the trie will shift when x is changed and the shifts will change the minimum number of accesses.

Applying the 80-20 rule to CC (coalescing list) for $\alpha = 1$ and b = 2 yields

$$\tilde{C}_I(1,2,.2,.8) = 1.336.$$

This value is less than the value for $\bar{C}_I(1,2)$ in figure 8.3.

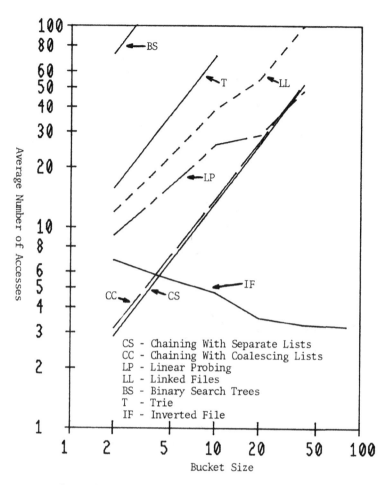

Figure 8.1. Mean Number of Accesses For A Retrieval

Operation Load Factor $\alpha = 1$

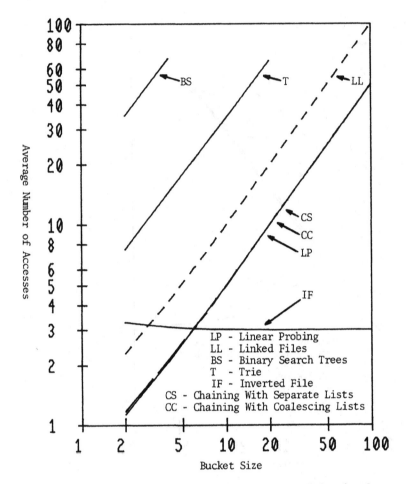

Figure 8.2. Mean Number of Accesses For A Retrieval
Operation Load Factor α = .5

8.2.4.   Deletion Time

The comparison is $\overline{F}(CS:CC:LP:BS:T:IF:LL,\ D,\ (150000000,$

$d,\ 1\ ))$ and $\overline{F}(CS:CC:LP:BS:T:IF:LL,\ D,\ (150000000,\ d,\ .5\ )).$

The time spent deleting items using the various methods are

illustrated in figure 8.5 and figure 8.6. This is a factor that must

be considered seriously if a large number of deletions are premitted

in a file. The minimum points again indicate the region where one

method is superior to another.

8.2.5.   Storage Space Requirements

In many problems the storage space requirement is critical.

The storage requirement in words is presented in this section for

chaining with separate lists, chaining with coalescing lists, linear

probing, linked files, inverted file, binary search tree and the

trie.

For the inverted file and the trie assume that one percent

of the keys are distinct. Assume that the keys are equally likely to

occur. The inverted file is characterized by 1,500,000 keys. The

storage requirement for the inverted file includes storage for the

file, directory and the inverted list. In the trie assume an average

of seven elements possible in each key position and the average

number of elements used in each position is five. Let h be two.

Table 8.1 illustrates the amount of storage required by binary search

tree, trie, linear probe and the inverted file method.

The average amount of storage for the other methods vary

with the load factor and bucket size. A comparison is illustrated in

figure 8.7 and figure 8.8.

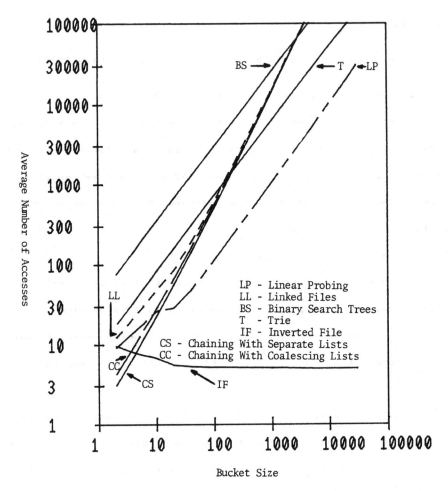

Figure 8.3.   Mean Number of Accesses for An Insertion

Operation Load Factor   α = 1

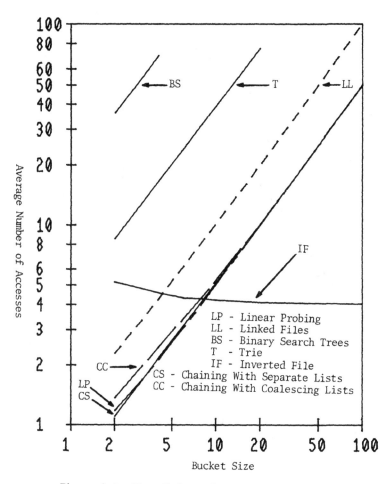

Figure 8.4.   Mean Number of Accesses For An Insertion

Operation Load Factor $\alpha = .5$

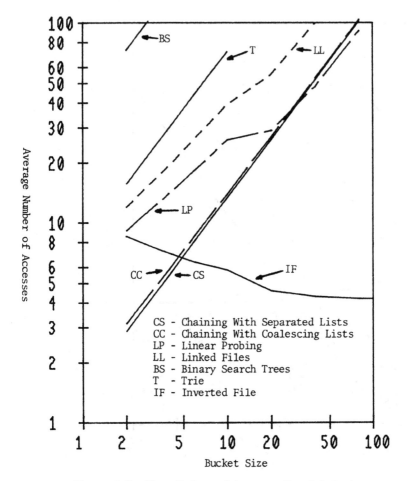

Figure 8.5. Mean Number of Accesses For A Deletion

Operation Load Factor α = 1

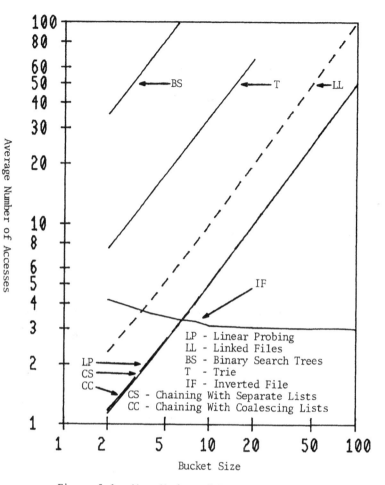

Figure 8.6.   Mean Number of Accesses For A Deletion

Operation Load Factor α = .5

TABLE 8.1

STORAGE REQUIREMENTS

BINARY SEARCH TREE, TRIE, LINEAR PROBE, INVERTED FILE

Method	Space
1. Binary Search Tree................	150000000
2. Trie...........................	63000000
3. Linear Probe...................	150000000
4. Inverted File...................	10151500000

A product performance measure is the product of the average number of accesses and the storage requirement. Figure 8.9 and figure 8.10 illustrates the product of the average number of accesses for a retrieval and the average storage requirement. These measurements are useful when considering accesses and storage requirements.

The retrieval times are generated using a unique key assumption in every method but the inverted file method. The product storage requirement and retrieval accesses for the other methods must be adjusted for identical keys in all comparisons. The average number of identical keys in an inverted file bucket is $\bar{O}(\alpha,b)$. Assume that the other methods are modified to retrieve identical keys. The adjustment for the comparison is the product of the average storage requirement and $\bar{O}(\alpha,b)$. A good approximation to $\bar{O}(\alpha,b)$ is αb.

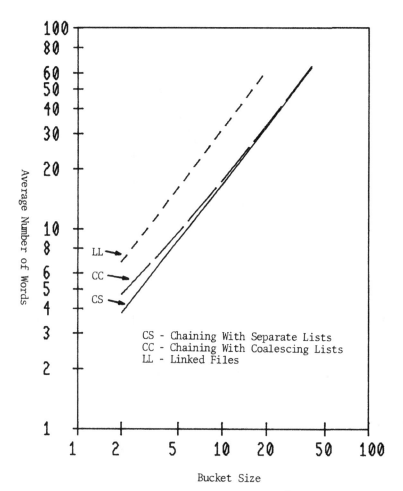

Figure 8.7.   Storage Requirements x 10^8 Words

Load Factor $\alpha = 1$

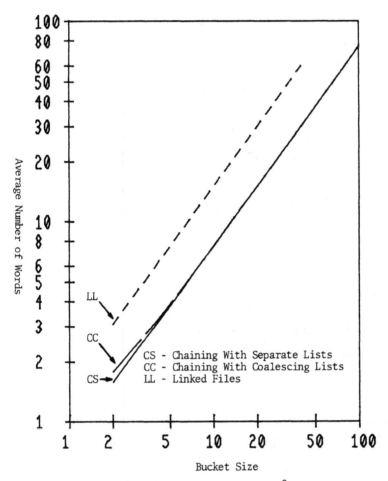

Figure 8.8. - Storage Requirements x 10^8 Words

Load Factor α = .5

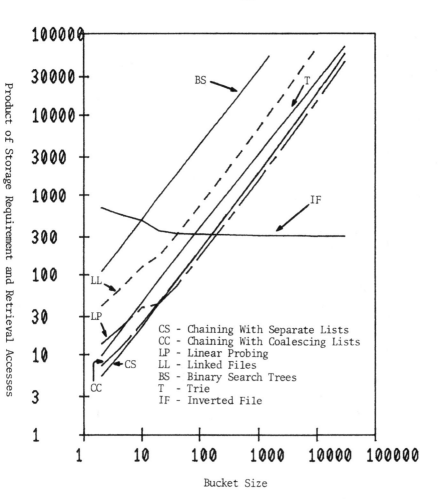

Figure 8.9. Product of Storage Requirement and Retrieval

Accesses x 10^8 Words

Load Factor $\alpha = 1$

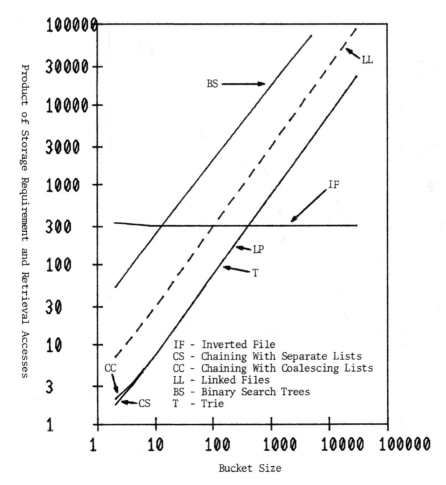

Figure 8.10. Product of Storage Requirement and

Retrieval Accesses x 10^8 Words

Load Factor α = .5

8.2.6.   Variable_Length_Keys

Several methods are useful in storing and retrieving variable length keys. The TRIE method and the Multidimensional Binary Search Trees introduced by Bentley [9] are good for variable length keys. The inverted file is excellent for variable length keys and is used in many cases.

8.2.7.   Fixed_Length_Keys

All methods that are efficient for variable length keys are efficient for fixed length keys, but the converse is not true. The methods can be ranked for fixed length keys. The trie and binary search trees are among the best methods considered in this monograph.

The trie is excellent for fixed length keys. In the trie, storage space is saved by restricting key lengths. Tree storage is saved by reducing the space to a fixed length for keys stored in the tree. This improves the efficiency in utilizing storage space. In many cases the inefficient utilization of storage space is compensated by high speed in both storage and retrieval.

8.2.8.   Hybrid_Methods

Any method composed of more than one search method is called a hybrid_method. Severance [63, 64] introduced a hybrid method called a TRIE-TREE. In this method the search for any item was done in two stages. One stage of search in the TRIE and a second stage of search in the TREE.

The linked file structure is a hybrid structure called a Linear Probe-Chaining with Separate Lists. The search of the directory is a Linear Probe and the search of the item file list is a Chain with Separate Lists method.

CHAPTER 9

CONCLUSIONS

9.1.   Conclusions

Several methods have been introduced and formulated to
store and retrieve items on a direct access storage device. Care has
been taken in the formulations to unify the notation in the various
methods. The methods have been presented in a modular manner to
allow comparisons of combinations of methods.

The effects of the methods and their data structures have
been studied and have been presented by tables to show the
interrelationships and tradeoffs available when using each method.

Algorithms have been presented and analyzed for a very
large data base using hash chaining with separate lists, hash
chaining with coalescing lists, hash linear probing, linked files,
inverted files, binary search trees, and the trie. The comparative
results have been presented in graphs. A mixture distribution has
been defined to apply the 80-20 rule using the various methods.

Figure 8.1, figure 8.2, figure 8.5, and figure 8.6 indicate
that the linear probing method is superior to the hash chaining
methods presented for retrieval and deletions for cases where the
buckets are approximately 50 percent full. When the buckets are 100
percent full and the bucket size is less than approximately 40, the

linear probing method requires more accesses than the chaining with separate lists and chaining with coalescing lists method.

Figure 8.3 and figure 8.4 indicate that the linear probing method require fewer accesses than the chaining methods presented for insertion cases where the buckets are approximately 50 percent full. When the buckets are 100 percent full and the bucket size is less than approximately 20, the linear probing method requires more accesses than the chaining with separate lists and chaining with coalescing lists methods.

Chaining with separate lists requires fewer than or equal the same number of accesses to the direct access storage device as chaining with coalescing lists. As the list lengths and load factor increase, the number of accesses using the chaining with coalescing lists method approaches the number of accesses for chaining with separate lists.

The storage requirements for chaining with separate lists, chaining with coalescing lists and linear probing are different. The linear probing method requires no overflow area. The chaining with separate list method tends to waste storage. To achieve maximum speed we would like to make the size of the buckets large, but when the size of the buckets is large, many of the lists will be empty and much of the storage space for the list will be wasted. The chaining with coalescing lists method avoids the storage waste encountered when using the chaining with separate lists method. The record storage and list heads are allowed to overlap. This allows a total of N records and N links instead of N records and $N + N$ links.

A sequential track allocation method has been presented to store a TREE and a TRIE. Algorithms have been presented and analyzed to retrieve, insert, and delete records using the sequential track allocation method.

Figure 8.1, figure 8.2, figure 8.3, figure 8.4, figure 8.5 and figure 8.6 indicate the relationship between the average number of accesses to the direct access storage device for the TREE and the TRIE. The average number of accesses required to access the direct access storage device for a TREE is greater than the average number of accesses required for a TRIE in a retrieval, insertion, and deletion operation. For retrieval and deletion with the buckets 50 percent and 100 percent full the binary search tree and the trie require more accesses than chaining with separate lists, chaining with coalescing lists and linear probing.

When the buckets are 100 percent full and the bucket size is approximately greater than 100, the Trie requires fewer accesses than chaining with separate lists and chaining with coalescing lists. The binary search tree requires fewer accesses than chaining with separate lists and chaining with coalescing lists for bucket sizes approximately greater than 1500. In all cases linear probing requires fewer accesses than both the trie and the binary search tree. When the buckets are 50 percent full, the binary search tree and the trie require a greater number of accesses.

The storage requirement for the TREE is the same order of magnitude as linear probing, assuming that a word is large enough to hold the record and two links. A TRIE requires more storage than chaining with separate list, chaining with coalescing lists and linear probing.

The linked files are presented as a hybrid of the linear probing and chaining with separate lists method. Algorithms have been presented and analyzed for retrieval, insertion and deletion. In all cases, the linked files require a greater number of accesses than chaining with separate lists, chaining with coalescing lists and linear probing. For retrieval and deletion the linked files require fewer accesses than the binary search tree and the trie.

When the buckets are 100 percent full the linked files require fewer accesses than the trie for bucket sizes up to approximately 100. The linked files require fewer accesses than the binary search tree for bucket sizes up to approximately 1500. When the buckets are 50 percent full the linked files require fewer accesses than the binary search tree and the trie.

The hybrid linked files require more storage than chaining with separate lists, chaining with coalescing lists and linear probing. Assume that a word is large enough to hold a record and two links for a binary search tree. The linked files require more storage than the binary search tree and less storage than the trie.

Algorithms have been presented and analyzed for an inverted file. Assume the index is searched using linear probing. The average number of accesses to retrieve a record with the bucket size gerater than four and the buckets 50 percent or 100 percent full, using the inverted file, is less than the average number of accesses for chaining with separate lists, chaining with coalescing lists, linear probing and the hybrid linked file method. In a retrieval, the number of accesses is always less than the number of accesses for a binary search tree and a trie.

When the buckets are 100 percent full and the bucket size is 2, the inverted file requires more accesses to insert a record than chaining with separate lists, chaining with coalescing lists, linear probing, linked file and the trie. The binary search tree requires more accesses in this case for all bucket sizes. When inserting a record, the inverted file requires fewer accesses than chaining with separate lists, chaining with coalescing lists and linked files for bucket sizes greater than approximately six. Fewer accesses are required to insert a record in an inverted file than a trie with bucket sizes greater than 2.

Consider the case where the buckets are 50 percent full. The average number of accesses to insert a record in the inverted file with bucket sizes greater than ten is less than the average number of accesses for chaining with separate lists, chaining with coalescing lists, linear probing and the linked file method. For all bucket sizes, the inverted file requires fewer accesses to insert a record than the binary search tree and the trie.

An inverted file with the buckets 100 percent full and the bucket size greater than five requires less accesses to delete a record than chaining with separate lists, chaining with coalescing lists, linear probing and the linked file method. Fewer accesses are required by the inverted file than the trie to delete a record for bucket sizes greater than 2.

When the buckets are 50 percent full and the bucket sizes are greater than nine the inverted file requires fewer accesses to delete a record than chaining with separate lists, chaining with coalescing lists, linear probing, linked files and the trie. In this case the binary search tree requires more accesses to delete a record.

The storage requirement for the inverted file includes storage for the file, inverted list and the index. When the bucket size is greater than 10000, this method requires less storage than every method presented.

The choice of which method is best depends on the type of data and the operations on that data. The performance measures presented in this monograph indicate where one method is good for a particular operation.

This analysis is important to designers of systems using very large data bases. The approach taken will aid the designer in selecting the correct data structure and search algorithms for processing very large data bases.

APPENDIX A

GLOSSARY OF TERMS

The following notation is used consistently throughout:

SYMBOL	MEANING
α	The load factor.
AVAIL	A link variable or link vector that points to BUCKET.
b	The bucket size.
BUCKET	An available storage pool.
$\beta(k;N,\frac{1}{d})$	Binomial probability distribution.
CC	Chaining with coalescing lists.
CS	Chaining with separate lists.
$\bar{c}_D(\alpha,b)$	Average number of accesses in a deletion operation.
$\bar{c}_I(\alpha,b)$	Average number of accesses in an insertion operation.
$\bar{c}_R(\alpha,b)$	Average number of accesses in a retrieval operation.
$\tilde{c}_\delta(\alpha,b,x,y)$	The expected value of the mixture

SYMBOL	MEANING
	probability distribution.
$\delta = \begin{cases} D \\ I \\ R \end{cases}$	Deletion operation. Insertion operation. Retrieval operation.
d	The number of buckets.
DL	A double linked file.
E(X)	The expected value of the variable X.
f	A function that transforms track addresses into internal main memory addresses.
$\bar{F}$(CS:CC, R, (N,d,α))	Comparison operator.
g(j)	A frequency function of the occurrence of items in a file.
Γ(x)	Gamma function.
h	The height or the level of a tree.
h(K)	A key-to-address transformation.
H(N,s)	The Nth harmonic number of order s.
K	A key.
LL	Linked file.
LP	Linear probing.
$\bar{L}_t$(m,b)	Average load time for a file.
m	The average number of records assigned to a bucket.
N	The number of records.
n	Average number of digits or characters possible in a key.
OVAIL	A link variable that points to OVERFLOW.

SYMBOL	MEANING
OVERFLOW	An overflow available storage pool.
$\bar{0}(m,b)$	Mean number of items in the buckets of an inverted file.
$p(J,\theta)$	A probability distribution that is Uniform when $\theta = 1$, Zipfian when $\theta = 0$ and approximately 80-20 when $\theta = \frac{\log .80}{\log .20}$.
$P(k)$	A probability distribution.
READ(P)	Read a track containing the address P.
READ P s	Read the record at P into the internal main memory buffer s.
RL	A ring list.
$S_s(n,b)$	Total storage required for an inverted file.
T	A trie.
WRITE(P)	Write a track containing the address P.
WRITE P s	Write the record in the internal main memory buffer s into the location starting at address P.
ω_c	Average storage requirement for chaining with separate lists.
ω_f	Average storage requirement for a linked file.
ω_l	Average storage requirement for chaining with coalescing lists.
ω_{ll}	Average storage requirement for a double linked file.
ω_p	Storage requirement for linear probing.

SYMBOL	MEANING
ω_s	Storage requirement for a tree.
ω_t	Average number of nodes required to store a trie.
x	Average number of digits or characters used in each position of a trie.
ϵ	80-20 rule.
μ	Uniform distribution.
z	Zipf's Law.
$\leftarrow$	Assign a value to a variable.
$\rightleftharpoons$	Assign a link variable a value and manage the available storage pool.

NODE OPERATORS	MEANING
ADATA	Address of the data.
ANEXT	Address of the next filial set.
ATAG	A tag indicating the state of an ANEXT node.
CODE	Code indicating the state of a node.
ENEXT	Address of the sibling.
ETAG	A tag indicating the state of an ENEXT node.
GET	Read input.
HEAD	List head.
INFO	Stored key.
NODE	Count of the bucket size.
PUT	Write output.
TAG	Bit tag to indicate a bucket node state.

REFERENCES

1. Abd-Alla, A.M. and Meltzer, A.C. *Principles of Digital Computer Design*, Volume 1 (1975).

2. Ackerman, A.F. "Quadratic Search for Hash Tables of Size p^n", *Comm ACM*, 17,3 (Feb. 1970) pp. 164.

3. Bays, C. "The Reallocation of Hash-Coded Tables", *Comm ACM*, 16,1 (Jan. 1973) pp. 11-14.

4. Bayer, R. and McCreight, E. "Organization and Maintenance of Large Ordered Indexes", *Acta Informatica*, 1 (1972) pp. 173-189.

5. Bayer, R. "Symmetric Binary B-Trees: Data Structure and Maintenance Algorithms", *Acta Informatica*, 1 (1972) pp. 290-306.

6. Bell, J.R. "The Quadratic Quotient Method: A Hash Code Eliminating Secondary Clustering", *Comm ACM*, 13,2 (Feb. 1970) pp. 107-109.

7. Bell, J.R. and Kaman, C.H. "The Linear Quotient Hash Code", *Comm ACM*, 13,11 (Nov. 1970) pp. 675-677.

8. Benner, F.H. "On Designing Generalized File Records for Management Information Systems", *AFIPS Conference Proceedings - 1967 Fall Joint Computer Conference*, 31, pp. 291-303.

9. Bentley, J.L. "Multidimensional Binary Search Trees Used for Associative Searching", *Comm ACM*, 18,9 (Sep. 1975) pp. 509-517.

10. Bloom, B.H. "Some Techniques and Trade-offs Affecting Large Data Base Retrieval Times", Proceedings - 1969 ACM National Conference, pp. 83-95.

11. Bloom, B.H. "Space/Time Trade-offs in Hash Coding With Allowable Errors", Comm ACM, 13,7 (July 1970) pp. 422-426.

12. Brent, R.P. "Reducing the Retrieval Time of Scatter Storage Techniques". Comm ACM, 16,2 (Feb. 1973) pp. 105-109.

13. Buchholz, W. "File Organization and Addressing", IBM Systems Journal, (June 1963) pp. 86-111.

14. Burkhard, W.A. "Some Approaches to Best-Match File Searching", Comm ACM, 16,4 (April 1973) pp. 230-236.

15. Clampett, Jr., H.A. "Randomized Binary Searching with Tree Structures", Comm ACM, 7,3 (March 1964) pp. 163-165.

16. Coffman, Jr., E.G. and Eve, J. "File Structures Using Hashing Functions", Comm ACM, 13,7 (July 1970) pp. 427-436.

17. Collmeyer, A.J. and Shemer, J.E. "Analysis of Retrieval for Selected File Organization Techniques", AFIPS Conference Proceedings - 1970 Fall Joint Computer Conference, pp. 201-210.

18. Day, A.C. "Full Table Quadratic Searching for Scatter Storage", Comm ACM, 13,8 (Aug. 1970) pp. 481-482.

19. de la Briandais, R. "File Searching Using Variable Length Keys" Proceeding - 1959 Western Joint Computing Conference, pp. 295-298.

20. Dodd, G.G. "Elements of Data Management Systems", Computing Surveys, 1,2 (June 1969) pp. 117-133.

21. Feller, W. An Introduction to Probability Theory and its Applications, Volume 1, John Wiley and Sons, Inc. (1950).

22. Finkel, R.A. and Bentley, J.L. "Quad Trees a Data Structure

for Retrieval on Composite Keys", _Acta Informatica_, 4 (1974) pp. 1-9.

23. Foster, C.C. "A Generalization of AVL Trees", _Comm ACM_, 16,8 (Aug. 1973) pp. 513-517.

24. Fredkin, E. "Trie Memory", _Comm ACM_, 3 (1960) pp. 490-499.

25. Ghosh, S.P. and Senko, M.E. "File Organization: On the Selection of Random Access Index Points for Sequential Files", _J. ACM_, 16,4 (Oct. 1969) pp. 569-579.

26. Gotlieb, C.C. and Tompa, F.W. "Choosing a Storage Schema", _Acta Informatica_, 3 (1974) pp. 297-319.

27. Heising, W.P. "Note on Random Addressing Techniques", _IBM Systems Journal_, (June 1963) pp. 111-116.

28. Hellerman, H. "Multidimensional Arrays", _Comm ACM_, (1962) pp. 205-207.

29. Hibbard, T.N. "Some Combinatorial Properties of Certain Trees with Applications to Searching and Sorting", _J. ACM_, 9,1 (Jan. 1962) pp. 13-28.

30. Hsiao, D. and Harary, F. "A Formal System for Information Retrieval from Files", _Comm ACM_, 13,2 (Feb. 1970) pp. 67-73.

31. Hu, T.C. and Tucker, A.C. "Optimal Computer Search-Trees and Variable-length Alphabetical Codes", _SIAM J. Appl. Math._, 21,4 (Dec. 1971) pp. 514-532.

32. IBM corp. _Introduction to IBM System 370 Direct Access Storage Devices and Organization Methods (GC20-1649-8)_, White Plains, N. Y.: IBM corp., 1974, 94pp.

33. Johnson, L.R. "An Indirect Chaining Method for Addressing on Secondary Keys", _Comm ACM_, 4,5 (May 1961) pp. 218-222.

34. Knuth, D.E. _The Art of Computer Programming, Vol. 3: Sorting_

and Seaching, Addison-Wesley, pp. 389-700.

35. Knuth, D.E. The Art of Computing Programming, Vol. 1:
    Fundamental Algorithms, Addison-Wesley, pp. 228-606.

36. Knuth, D.E. "Optimum Binary Search Trees", Acta Informatica, 1
    (1971) pp. 14-25.

37. Landauer, W.I. "The Balanced Tree and its Utilization in
    Information Retrieval", IEEE Trans. Electron. Computers,
    EC-12,5 (Dec. 1963) pp. 863-871.

38. Lowe, T.C. "The Influence of Data Base Characteristics and
    Usage on Direct Access File Organization", J. ACM, 15,4
    (Oct. 1968) pp. 535-548.

39. Luccio, F. "Weighted Increment Linear Search for Scatter
    Tables", Comm ACM, 15,12 (Dec. 1972) pp. 1045-1047.

40. Lum, V.Y., Ling, H. and Senko, M. E. "Analysis of a Complex
    Data Management Access Method by Simulation Modeling",
    Proceeding -1970 Fall Joint Computer Conference, pp. 211-230.

41. Lum, V.Y., Yuen, P.S.T. and Dodd, M. "Key-to-Address Transform
    Techniques: A Fundamental Performance Study on Large Existing
    Formatted Files", Comm ACM, 14,4 (April 1971) pp. 228-239.

42. Lum, V.Y. and Yuen, P.S.T. "Additional Results on Key-to-
    Address Transform Techniques: A Fundamental Performance Study
    on Large Existing Formatted Files", Comm ACM, 15,11 (Nov. 1972)
    p. 996.

43. Lum, V.Y. "Multi-Attribute Retrieval with Combined Indexes",
    Comm ACM, 13,11 (Nov. 1970) pp. 660-665.

44. Maurer, W.D. "An Improved Hash Code for Scatter Storage",
    Comm ACM, 11,1 (Jan. 1968) pp. 35-38.

45. Maurer, W.D. and Lewis, T.G. "Hash Table Methods", Computing

Surveys, 7,1 (March 1975) pp. 5-19.

46. Maurer, W.D. PROGRAMMING: An Introduction To Computer
    Languages and Techniques, Holden-Day, Inc., pp. 74-88.

47. McIlroy, M.D. "A Variant Method of File Searching", _Comm ACM_,
    p. 101.

48. Morris, R. "Scatter Storage Techniques", _Comm ACM_, 11,1
    (Jan. 1968) pp. 38-44.

49. Morrison, D.R. "PATRICA-Practical Algorithm to Retrieve
    Information Coded in Alphanumeric", _J. ACM_, 15,4 (Oct. 1968)
    pp. 514-534.

50. Muntz, R. and Uzgalis, R. "Dynamic Storage Allocation
    for Binary Search Trees in a Two-Level Memory", _Proceedings
    - 1970 4th Princeton Conference on Information Science and
    Systems_, pp. 345-349.

51. Nievergett, J. and Reingold, E.M. "Binary Search Trees of
    Bounded Balance", _SIAM J. Computing_, 2,1 (March 1973)
    pp. 33-43.

52. Nievergelt, J. "Binary Search Trees and File Organization",
    Computing Surveys, 6,3 (Sept. 1974) pp. 195-207.

53. Olson, C.A. "Random Access File Organization for Indirectly
    Addressed Records", _Proceedings - 1969 ACM National Conference_,
    pp. 539-549.

54. Peterson, W.W. "Addressing for Random Access Storage",
    IBM Journal of Research and Development, 1 (April 1957)
    pp. 130-146.

55. van der Pool, J.A. "Optimum Storage Allocation for Initial
    Loading of a File", _IBM J. Research and Development_, (1972)
    pp. 579-586.

56. van der Pool, J. A. "Optimum Storage Allocation for a File in
     Steady State", IBM J. Research and Development, (Jan. 1973)
     pp. 27-38.

57. Prywes, N.S. Critical Factors in Data Management, Prentice-
     Hall, Inc. pp. 127-146.

58. Radke, C.E. "The use of Quadratic Residue Research", Comm ACM,
     31,1 (Feb. 1970) pp. 105-107.

59. Rivest, R.L. "Partial-Match Retrieval Algorithms", SIAM J.
     Computing, 5,1 (March 1976) pp. 19-50.

60. Salton, G. Dynamic Information and Library Processing,
     Prentice-Hall, Inc. (1975) pp. 277-320.

61. Schay, G. and Spruth, W.G. "Analysis of a File Addressing
     Method", Comm ACM, 5,8 (Aug. 1962) pp. 459-462.

62. Scidmore, A.K. and Weinberg, B.L. "Storage and Search
     Properties of a Tree-Organized Memory System", Comm ACM,
     6,1 (Jan. 1963) pp. 28-31.

63. Severance, D. Some Generalized Modeling Structures for
     use in Design of File Organizations, Ph.D. Dissertation,
     The University Of Michigan, 1972.

64. Severance, D. "Identifier Search Mechanisms: A Survey and
     Generalized Model", Computing Surveys, 6,3 (Sep. 1974)
     pp. 175-194.

65. Severance, D. and Duhne, R. "A Practitioner's Guide
     to Addressing Algorithms", Comm ACM, 19,6 (June 1976)
     pp. 314-326.

66. Sussenguth, Jr., E.H. "Use of Tree Structures for Processing
     Files", Comm ACM, 6,5 (May 1963) pp. 272-279.

67. Tainiter, M. "Addressing for Random-Access Storage with

Multiple Bucket Capacities", J. ACM. (1963) pp. 307-315.

68. Ullman, J.D. "A Note on the Efficiency of Hashing Functions",
    J. ACM. 19,3 (July 1972) pp.569-575.

69. Wedekind, H. "On The Selection of Access Paths in a Data Base
    System", Proceedings - 1974 IFIP Working Conference on Data
    Base Management. pp. 385-397.

70. Williams, F.A. "Handling Identifiers as Internal Symbols in
    Language Processors", Comm ACM. 2,6 (June 1959) pp. 21-24.

71. Zipf, G.K. Human Behavior and The Principle of Least Effort.
    Hafner Publishing Company, (1965).